T0364555

AQA GCSE (9–1)
Physics

Grade 6–7 Booster Workbook

Gillian Lindsey
Lynn Pharaoh

William Collins' dream of knowledge for all began with the publication of his first book in 1819. A self-educated mill worker, he not only enriched millions of lives, but also founded a flourishing publishing house. Today, staying true to this spirit, Collins books are packed with inspiration, innovation and practical expertise. They place you at the centre of a world of possibility and give you exactly what you need to explore it.

Collins. Freedom to teach.

Published by Collins
An imprint of HarperCollins*Publishers*
The News Building
1 London Bridge Street
London
SE1 9GF

HarperCollins*Publishers*
Macken House
39/40 Mayor Street Upper
Dublin 1
DO1 C9W8
Ireland

Browse the complete Collins catalogue at
www.collins.co.uk

© HarperCollins*Publishers* Limited 2019

10 9 8 7 6 5

ISBN 978-0-00-832256-4

All rights reserved. No part of this publication may be reproduced, stored in a retrieval system, or transmitted in any form by any means, electronic, mechanical, photocopying, recording or otherwise, without the prior written permission of the Publisher or a licence permitting restricted copying in the United Kingdom issued by the Copyright Licensing Agency Ltd, Barnard's Inn, 86 Fetter Lane, London, EC4A 1EN.

British Library Cataloguing-in-Publication Data
A catalogue record for this publication is available from the British Library.

Authors: Gillian Lindsey, Lynn Pharaoh
Expert reviewer: Neil Crumpton
Development editor: Gillian Lindsey
Commissioning editors: Rachael Harrison & Jennifer Hall
In-house editor: Alexandra Wells
Copyeditor: David Hemsley
Proof reader: Pete Robinson
Answer checker: Peter Batty
Cover designers: The Big Mountain Design & Creative Direction
Cover photos: bl: Sdecoret/Shutterstock, tr: Respiro/Shutterstock
Typesetter and illustrator: Jouve India Private Limited
Production controller: Katharine Willard
Printed and bound by: Ashford Colour Press Ltd

This book contains FSC™ certified paper and other controlled sources to ensure responsible forest management.

For more information visit: www.harpercollins.co.uk/green

The publishers gratefully acknowledge the permission granted to reproduce the copyright material in this book. Every effort has been made to trace copyright holders and to obtain their permission for the use of copyright material. The publishers will gladly receive any information enabling them to rectify any error or omission at the first opportunity.

Contents

Introduction

This workbook will help you build your confidence in answering Physics questions for GCSE Physics and GCSE Combined Science.

It gives you practice in using key scientific words, writing longer answers and answering synoptic questions, as well as applying knowledge and analysing information.

You will find all the different question types in the workbook so you can get plenty of practice in providing short and long answers.

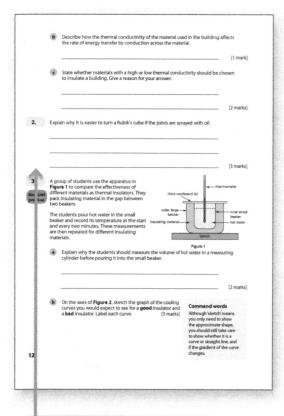

Learn how to answer test questions with annotated worked examples.

This will help you develop the skills you need to answer questions.

The questions also cover required practicals, maths skills and synoptic questions – look out for the tags which will help you to identify these questions.

Higher Tier content is clearly marked throughout.

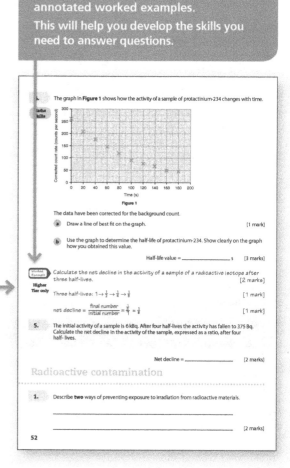

Select the correct equation from the Physics equations sheet.

Thermal energy transferred = _____ J   [2 marks]

b The electric hob transfers 420 000 J as thermal energy in the time taken to heat the water.

Calculate the efficiency of this method of heating water.

Give your answer as both a decimal and as a percentage.

Maths
Efficiency values can be given as decimals or percentages. Remember that percentages are fractions of 100. For example, 90% is the fraction $\frac{90}{100}$.

Efficiency as a decimal = _____

Efficiency as a percentage = _____   [2 marks]

Higher Tier only

c This method of heating water is not very efficient.

Suggest one way the efficiency of the energy transfer could be improved. Explain your answer.

Command words
When the question asks you to **suggest**, you must link what you already know to the information you are given.

_____

_____

_____

_____

_____   [3 marks]

4. Coal-fired power stations are not very efficient. A lot of the thermal energy released when the coal is burned is wasted. For example, the water used to cool the steam leaving the turbines increases its store of thermal energy. This water is in direct contact with the air and transfers energy to the thermal energy store in the air.

Higher Tier only

Suggest one way the efficiency of the power station could be improved. Explain your answer.

_____

_____

_____   [2 marks]

14

There are lots of hints and tips to help you out. Look out for tips on how to decode command words, key tips for required practicals and maths skills, and common misconceptions.

The amount of support gradually decreases throughout the workbook. As you build your skills you should be able to complete more of the questions yourself.

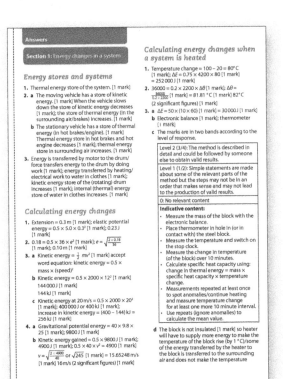

Physics equation sheet

It is important to be able to recall and apply the following equations using standard units:

Equation Number	Word Equation	Symbol Equation
1	weight = mass × gravitational field strength	$W = mg$
2	work done = force × distance (along the line of action of the force)	$W = Fs$
3	force applied to a spring = spring constant × extension	$F = ke$
4	moment of a force = force × distance (normal to direction of force)	$M = Fd$
5	pressure = $\frac{\text{force normal to a surface}}{\text{area of that surface}}$	$p = \frac{F}{A}$
6	distance travelled = speed × time	$s = vt$
7	acceleration = $\frac{\text{change in velocity}}{\text{time taken}}$	$a = \frac{\Delta v}{t}$
8	resultant force = mass × acceleration	$F = ma$
9	momentum = mass × velocity	$p = mv$
10	kinetic energy = 0.5 × mass × (speed)²	$E_k = \frac{1}{2}mv^2$
11	gravitational potential energy = mass × gravitational field strength × height	$E_p = mgh$
12	power = $\frac{\text{energy transferred}}{\text{time}}$	$P = \frac{E}{t}$
13	power = $\frac{\text{work done}}{\text{time}}$	$P = \frac{W}{t}$
14	efficiency = $\frac{\text{useful output energy transfer}}{\text{useful input energy transfer}}$	
15	efficiency = $\frac{\text{useful power output}}{\text{total power input}}$	
16	wave speed = frequency × wavelength	$v = f\lambda$
17	charge flow = current × time	$Q = It$
18	potential difference = current × resistance	$V = IR$
19	power = potential difference × current	$P = VI$
20	power = (current)² × resistance	$P = I^2R$

133

The 'Physics equation sheet' section is a helpful collection of all the equations you'll need to know by heart to do well on your exam. Also provided is a list the equations you will be given in the exam. You won't need to learn those by heart, but you will need to know which one to use, and be able to use it correctly.

There are answers to all the questions at the back of the book. You can check your answers yourself or your teacher might tear them out and give them to you later to mark your work.

3

Energy stores and systems

1. A teacher drops a book. The book lands on the floor and does not bounce.

    Which energy store has increased once the book is at rest on the floor?
    Tick **one** box.

    Kinetic energy store of the book ☐

    Gravitational potential energy store of the book ☐

    Thermal energy store of the system ☐　　　　　　　　　[1 mark]

2. When a vehicle slows down, energy is transferred from one store to another.

    Remember
    There are 3 marks here so you need to make three points. You must say more than just what the original and final energy stores are.

    a Describe the changes in energy stores as the vehicle slows down.

    _____

    _____

    _____ [3 marks]

    b The vehicle stops and the engine is turned off.

    Describe the changes in energy stores that occur over the next few minutes.

    _____

    _____

    _____ [3 marks]

3. The drum of a tumble dryer is a system that includes the drum, the clothes in the drum and the water in the clothes. A motor applies a force to turn the drum. An electric heater heats the drum.

    Describe the useful energy transfers that occur in the tumble dryer when the machine is switched on.

    _____

    _____

_____

_____ [4 marks]

Calculating energy changes

1. A force stretches a spring by 30.0 cm. The spring has a spring constant of 5.0 N/m. Calculate the elastic potential energy stored in the spring.

Maths Skills

Use the correct equation from the Physics equations sheet.

Energy stored = _____ J [3 marks]

Maths

The amount of elastic potential energy stored in a system is calculating using the following equation which is on the Physics equations sheet: $E_e = \frac{1}{2} ke^2$. You should be able to select and apply the equation.

A spring is compressed by 0.10 m increasing its elastic potential energy store by 0.1 J.

Calculate the spring constant of the spring in N/m. [3 marks]

Elastic potential energy: $E_e = \frac{1}{2} ke^2$

$0.1 = 0.5 \times k \times (0.10)^2$ [1 mark]

So $k = \dfrac{0.1}{0.5 \times (0.10)^2}$ [1 mark]

$= 20$ N/m [1 mark]

Remember

Whenever you substitute a value in an equation, check that the value has standard units. If not, convert the value before substituting into the equation. Extension must be in metres.

Remember

The equation for elastic potential energy can also be used to calculate the energy stored in a compressed spring. In this case, e represents the **decrease** in length of the spring.

2. A stretched spring stores 0.18 J of energy. The spring constant of the spring is 36 N/m.

Maths Skills

Calculate the extension of the spring. Use the correct equation from the Physics equations sheet.

Maths

To find the extension you'll need to rearrange the equation to put extension on its own, on one side of the equals sign. Think about what needs to be done to both sides of the equation to get extension on its own.

Extension = _____ m [3 marks]

3.

a Write down the equation that links kinetic energy to mass and speed.

_____ [1 mark]

b A van of mass 2000 kg is travelling at a speed of 12 m/s.

Calculate the van's store of kinetic energy.

Give your answer in kJ.

Kinetic energy = _____ kJ [3 marks]

c The van's speed increases to 20 m/s. Calculate the increase in the van's kinetic energy.

Increase in kinetic energy = _____ kJ [3 marks]

> **Maths**
> You need to learn the equations for kinetic energy and gravitational potential energy as they may not be given to you in the question.

4.

A child cycles uphill. The cyclist and her bike have a combined mass of 40 kg. The vertical height gained is 25 m.

a Calculate the increase in gravitational potential energy of the cyclist and her bike.

Gravitational field strength = 9.8 N/kg.

Gravitational potential energy = _____ J [2 marks]

b The child and her bike turn around and freewheel down the hill. As she freewheels down the hill, resistive forces on her body and the bike dissipate 50% of the stored gravitational potential energy to the surroundings.

Calculate the speed of the cyclist as she reaches the bottom of the hill.

Give your answer to 2 significant figures.

> **Maths**
> To round a number to 2 significant figures, look at the third digit. Round up if the digit is 5 or more. Round down if the digit is 4 or less.

Speed = _____ m/s [6 marks]

Calculating energy changes when a system is heated

1. An electric kettle is used to heat 750 g of water.

Calculate the thermal energy that must be transferred to the water to raise its temperature from 20 °C to boiling point. Select the correct equation from the Physics equations sheet.

Specific heat capacity of water = 4200 J/kg °C.

Thermal energy transferred = _____ J   [3 marks]

Maths

The equation for the energy change involved in raising and lowering the temperature of a system is $\Delta E = mc\Delta\theta$. This equation is on the Physics equations sheet. You need to be able to select and apply this equation.

Worked Example

The specific heat capacity of aluminium is 910 J/kg °C. A heater transfers 35 000 J to the thermal energy store of a 1.00 kg block of aluminium.

Calculate the temperature rise of the block. Select the correct equation from the Physics equations sheet.

Give your answer to 2 significant figures.   [4 marks]

$\Delta E = mc\Delta\theta$ so $35\,000 = 1.00 \times 910 \times \Delta\theta$ [1 mark]

$\Delta\theta = \frac{35\,000}{1.00 \times 910}$ [1 mark]

$= 38.46\,°C$ [1 mark]

$= 38\,°C$ (to 2 significant figures)   [1 mark]

2. A stove transfers 36 000 J to the thermal energy store of vegetable oil in a frying pan. The oil has a mass of 0.2 kg and a specific heat capacity of 2200 J/kg °C.

Calculate the increase in temperature of the oil. Select the correct equation from the Physics equations sheet.

Give your answer to 2 significant figures.

Temperature rise = _____ °C   [4 marks]

3.

A student heats a steel block using an electrical heater. The heater transfers energy to the thermal energy store of the block at a rate of 50 J each second.

Required practical

The student switches the heater on for exactly 10 minutes.

a Calculate the thermal energy transferred to the block in this time.

Energy transferred = _____ J   [2 marks]

b State what **two** other pieces of apparatus the student needs to make measurements to calculate the specific heat capacity of steel.

1 _____

2 _____   [2 marks]

c Describe how the apparatus could be used to determine the specific heat capacity of steel.

_____

_____

_____

_____

_____

_____

_____

_____   [4 marks]

d The value of specific heat capacity the student calculates using this method is greater than the true value.

Explain why.

_____

_____

_____   [2 marks]

Work and power

1. State the unit of power.

_____ [1 mark]

Maths

You need to learn these two equations for power as they may not be given to you in the question:

$$power = \frac{energy\ transferred}{time},$$

$$power = \frac{work\ done}{time}$$

2. An electric kettle boils 1 kg water. Another kettle has twice the power rating. How long will this kettle take to boil the same mass of water, compared to the first kettle?

_____ [1 mark]

3. A 20 W light bulb is switched on for 2 hours. How much energy is transferred by the electric current in this time?

Maths Skills

Energy transferred = _____ J   [2 marks]

Worked Example

A boy of mass 50 kg runs up some steps in 3.5 s. The vertical height gained is 5.0 m. Calculate his power.

Gravitational field strength = 9.8 N/kg.   [4 marks]

Gravitational potential energy gained = 50 × 9.8 × 5.0   [1 mark]

= 2450 J   [1 mark]

The work done is the increase in the boy's gravitational potential energy, so

$$power = \frac{work\ done}{time} = \frac{2450}{3.5}$$ [1 mark]

= 700 W   [1 mark]

4. An electric car of mass 1200 kg accelerates from rest to a speed of 15.0 m/s in 10.0 s.

Maths Skills

Calculate its power.

Power = _____ W   [4 marks]

5. The Montparnasse in Paris has one of the fastest lifts in the world. The journey to the viewing platform raises passengers 196 m above ground in 38 s.

Maths Skills

If the lift and its passengers have a combined mass of 1050 kg, calculate the power of the lift's motor.

Give your answer to 2 significant figures.

Gravitational field strength = 9.8 N/kg.

Power = _____ W   [5 marks]

Conservation of energy

1. When an electric motor raises a weight, work is done and energy is transferred to the gravitational potential energy store of the weight. State what happens to the energy that is **not** usefully transferred.

_____   [1 mark]

2. A wind turbine transfers energy from the kinetic energy store of moving air to an electric current produced in a generator.

For every 500 J in the moving air's kinetic energy store, only 120 J is usefully transferred to the current in the generator.

Explain how energy is conserved in this situation.

_____

_____

_____   [3 marks]

3. A cyclist is travelling at a steady speed along a flat road. When she stops pedalling, the bike gradually slows down and stops.

Explain what happens to the kinetic energy store of the cyclist and her bike when she stops pedalling.

_____

_____

_____

_____

_____

_____

_____

_____ [4 marks]

Literacy

For answers to 4- and 6-mark extended written questions, don't simply write down everything you know. You need to make logical links between your sentences to get full marks.

4. A football of mass of 0.450 kg is kicked from the ground to a height of 2.3 m. The ball then falls under gravity.

Maths Skills

Calculate the speed of the ball as it hits the ground. Ignore the effect of air resistance.

Gravitational field strength = 9.8 N/kg.

Give your answer to 2 significant figures.

Problem solving

In a 5- or 6-mark calculation question, there is usually more than one problem to solve to get the information needed to calculate the final answer. Always show your working. You may still get some marks even if the final answer is wrong.

Speed on hitting the ground = _____ m/s   [6 marks]

Ways of reducing unwanted energy transfers

1. Thermal energy stored in a heated building is transferred out of the building by conduction through the walls, floor, roof and windows.

a Explain why this is described as an **unwanted** energy transfer.

_____

_____ [2 marks]

b Describe how the thermal conductivity of the material used in the building affects the rate of energy transfer by conduction across the material.

_____ [1 mark]

c State whether materials with a high or low thermal conductivity should be chosen to insulate a building. Give a reason for your answer.

_____

_____ [2 marks]

2. Explain why it is easier to turn a Rubik's cube if the joints are sprayed with oil.

_____

_____

_____ [3 marks]

3.

Required practical

A group of students use the apparatus in **Figure 1** to compare the effectiveness of different materials as thermal insulators. They pack insulating material in the gap between two beakers.

The students pour hot water in the small beaker and record its temperature at the start and every two minutes. These measurements are then repeated for different insulating materials.

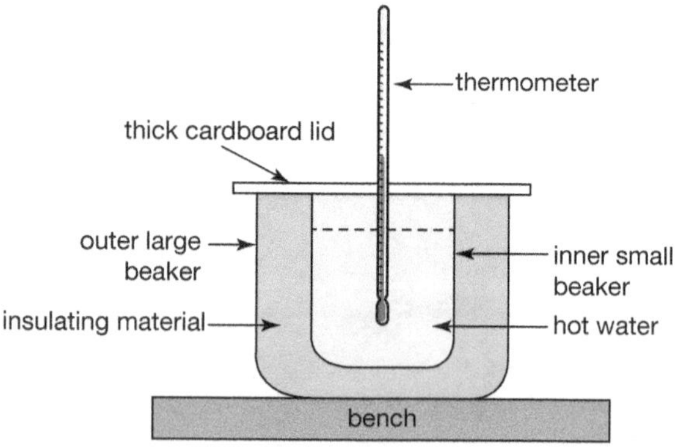

thermometer
thick cardboard lid
outer large beaker
inner small beaker
insulating material
hot water
bench

Figure 1

a Explain why the students should measure the volume of hot water in a measuring cylinder before pouring it into the small beaker.

_____

_____ [2 marks]

b On the axes of **Figure 2**, sketch the graph of the cooling curves you would expect to see for a **good** insulator and a **bad** insulator. Label each curve.   [3 marks]

Command words

Although 'sketch' means you only need to show the approximate shape, you should still take care to show whether it is a curve or straight line, and if the gradient of the curve changes.

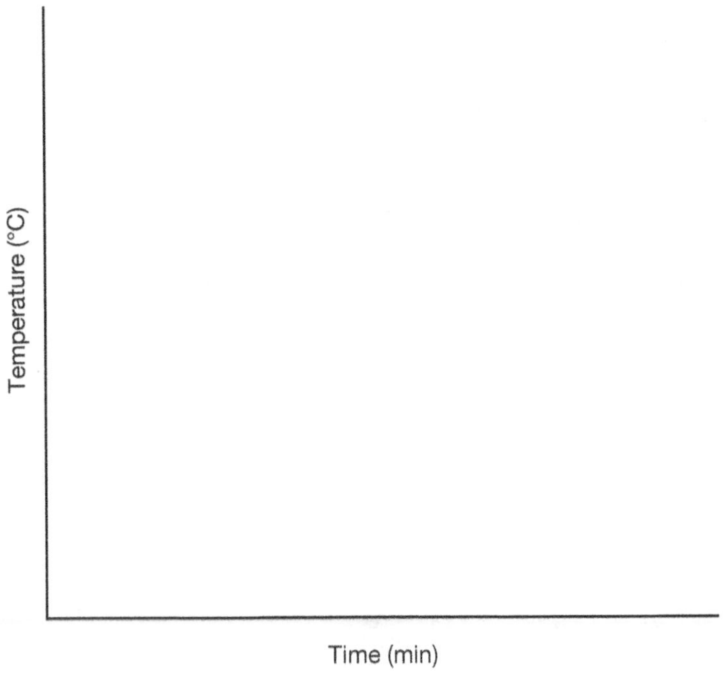

Maths

The steeper the gradient of a temperature versus time graph, the quicker the temperature is changing.

Temperature (°C)

Time (min)

Figure 2

Efficiency

1. Write down the equation that links the efficiency of an energy transfer to the total input energy and the useful output energy.

Maths

You need to remember the equations for efficiency as they may not be given to you in the question.

_____ [1 mark]

2. A diesel car engine is 40% efficient. Describe what is meant by 40% efficient.

_____

_____ [1 mark]

3. An electric hob is used to heat 0.90 kg of water in a pan.

Maths Skills

Synoptic

a Calculate the thermal energy that must be transferred to the water to raise its temperature from 18 °C to 98 °C.

Specific heat capacity of water = 4200 J/kg °C.

Select the correct equation from the Physics equations sheet.

Thermal energy transferred = _____ J   [2 marks]

b The electric hob transfers 420 000 J as thermal energy in the time taken to heat the water.

Calculate the efficiency of this method of heating water.

Give your answer as both a decimal and as a percentage.

Maths

Efficiency values can be given as decimals or percentages. Remember that percentages are fractions of 100. For example, 90% is the fraction $\frac{90}{100}$.

Efficiency as a decimal = _____

Efficiency as a percentage = _____   [2 marks]

Higher Tier only

c This method of heating water is not very efficient.

Suggest one way the efficiency of the energy transfer could be improved. Explain your answer.

Command words

When the question asks you to **suggest**, you must link what you already know to the information you are given.

_____

_____

_____

_____

_____   [3 marks]

4.

Higher Tier only

Coal-fired power stations are not very efficient. A lot of the thermal energy released when the coal is burned is wasted. For example, the water used to cool the steam leaving the turbines increases its store of thermal energy. This water is in direct contact with the air and transfers energy to the thermal energy store in the air.

Suggest one way the efficiency of the power station could be improved. Explain your answer.

_____

_____

_____   [2 marks]

National and global energy resources

1. Biofuels, wind, hydro-electricity, geothermal, the tides, the Sun and water waves are all renewable energy resources. Describe **one** difference in the way these energy resources can be used.

_____ [1 mark]

2. Suggest **two** reasons why many countries are trying to reduce the amount of non-renewable energy resources they use.

1 _____

2 _____ [2 marks]

3. Look at **Table 1**, which shows energy resource use trends in the UK.

Energy resource	% of total consumption 2013	% of total consumption 2014	% of total consumption 2015	% of total consumption 2016
coal	35.2	28.1	21.2	8.6
gas	26.8	29.3	28.9	41.7
nuclear	18.3	17.1	18.8	19.3
renewable	14.5	18.2	23.4	23.5

Table 1

The share of electricity supplied from coal fell from 2015 to 2016 due to closures of two large coal power stations in March 2016.

a Use the data to compare the trends in how the UK uses renewable energy resources and gas for generating electricity.

Literacy

A **trend** is a pattern in the data. Don't just say 'it goes up' or 'it goes down'. **Compare** the size of the increase or decrease using the data from the table.

_____

_____

_____

_____ [2 marks]

b Suggest an explanation for why these trends occurred.

_____

_____ [1 mark]

4. Compare the reliability of using wind power and nuclear fuel for generating electricity.

_____

_____

_____

_____ [2 marks]

Command words

A **compare** question means give similarities and differences. You will need to mention both parts in the comparison.

5. Compare the environmental effects of using wind power and nuclear fuel for generating electricity.

_____

_____

_____

_____

_____

_____

_____

_____

_____ [4 marks]

Circuit diagrams

1. Identify the circuit symbols in **Table 1**.

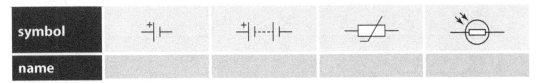

symbol				
name				

Table 1 [4 marks]

2. Complete **Table 2** by drawing the circuit symbols.

symbol			
name	fixed resistor	variable resistor	ammeter

Table 2 [3 marks]

3. Draw a circuit showing a cell and three lamps, each of which can be switched on and off independently.

[2 marks]

Electrical charge and current

Worked Example

2.0 C of charge flows through a resistor in 50 s.

Calculate the current through the resistor.

Give your answer in mA. [4 marks]

Using the equation $Q = It$

$$2.0 = I \times 50$$ [1 mark]

This can be rearranged to give

$$I = \frac{2.0}{50}$$ [1 mark]

$$= 0.040 \text{ A}$$ [1 mark]

$$= 40 \text{ mA}$$ [1 mark]

Remember

You need to learn the equation relating charge flow to current and time as it may not be given to you in the exam.

17

1. An electric circuit is shown in **Figure 1**.

a Write down the equation that links charge flow, current and time.

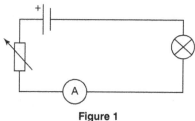

Figure 1

_____ [1 mark]

Maths Skills **b** The ammeter reads 0.020 A.

Calculate the charge that flows through the lamp in 100 s.

Charge = _____ C   [2 marks]

Maths Skills **c** The variable resistor is now adjusted so that the lamp becomes much dimmer.

It takes 100 s for 1.2 C to pass through the lamp.

Calculate the current through the lamp.

Give your answer in mA.

Current = _____ mA   [4 marks]

2. The reading on the ammeter in the circuit in **Figure 2** is 200 μA.

Maths Skills

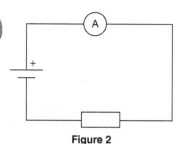

Figure 2

> **Remember**
>
> The size of an electric current is sometimes expressed in microamps (μA). 'micro' is a prefix which is equal to $\frac{1}{1\,000\,000}$. So 1 μA = 1×10^{-6} A.

Calculate the time taken for 1.0 C of charge to pass through the resistor.

Time = _____ s   [4 marks]

Electrical resistance

 Worked Example

The potential difference across a 120 Ω resistor is 6.0 V.

Calculate the current flowing through the resistor.

Give your answer in mA. [4 marks]

Remember

You need to learn the equation linking potential difference, current and resistance as it may not be given to you in the exam.

Using the equation $V = IR$

$$6.0 = I \times 120$$ [1 mark]

$$I = \frac{6.0}{120}$$ [1 mark]

$$= 0.050\,A$$ [1 mark]

$$= 50\,mA$$ [1 mark]

1. In a circuit, the potential difference across a 200 Ω resistor is 9.0 V. Calculate the current through the resistor.

Maths Skills Give your answer in mA.

Current = _____ mA [4 marks]

2. When the switch in the circuit in **Figure 3** is closed the ammeter reads 60 mA and the voltmeter reads 1.5 V.

Maths Skills Calculate the resistance of resistor R.

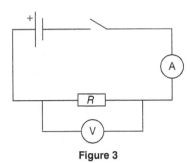

Resistance = _____ Ω [4 marks]

Figure 3

3. **a** A student is asked to determine the combined resistance of two unknown resistors connected in series as shown in **Figure 4**.

Required practical

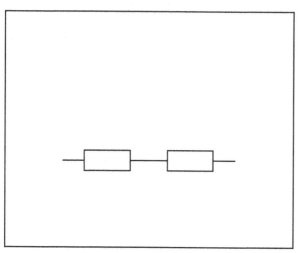

Figure 4

Draw on **Figure 4** the circuit that the student could use to determine the value of the combined resistance. [3 marks]

b Describe how the student should use the equipment in the circuit to determine the value of the combined resistance.

_____

_____ [2 marks]

4. A student uses the circuit shown in **Figure 5** to investigate how the resistance of a wire depends on its length.

Required practical

Before starting the investigation, the student made the following prediction:

> The resistance of the wire will be directly proportional to its length.

a The student measured the resistance of eight different lengths of wire.

All eight lengths had the same diameter.

Explain why it is important that the wires had the same diameter.

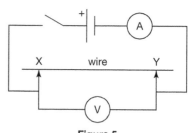

Figure 5

_____

_____

_____ [2 marks]

b Explain why it is important to make sure there are no kinks in the wire.

_____ [1 mark]

c Identify the dependent, independent and control variables.

Dependent variable: _____

Independent variable: _____

Control variable: _____ [3 marks]

d The graph shows the student's values of resistance for each of the eight lengths of wire. The student has drawn a line of best fit.

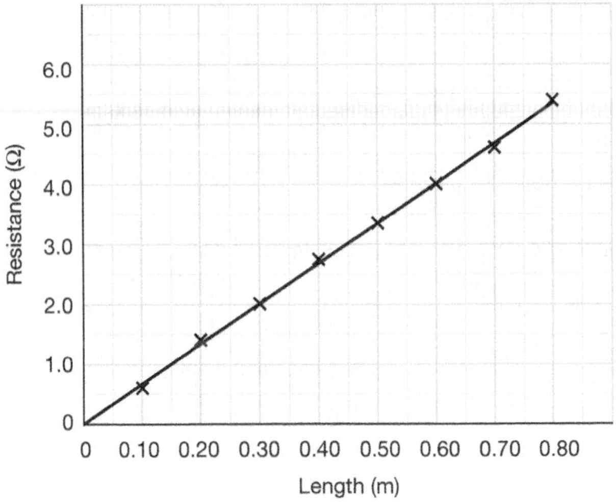

Figure 6

Give the range of lengths that the student used.

_____ [1 mark]

e Explain why the data plotted in **Figure 6** supports the student's prediction.

_____ [1 mark]

f Use the graph to predict the length of wire that would have a resistance of 1.6 Ω.

Length = _____ m [1 mark]

g The gradient of the graph is equal to the resistance per metre of the wire.

Determine the resistance per metre of the wire.

_____

Gradient = _____ Ω/m [1 mark]

Resistors and *I–V* characteristics

1. The circuit in **Figure 7** contains two circuit components labelled P and Q. When the switch is closed, the ammeter records a current in the circuit.

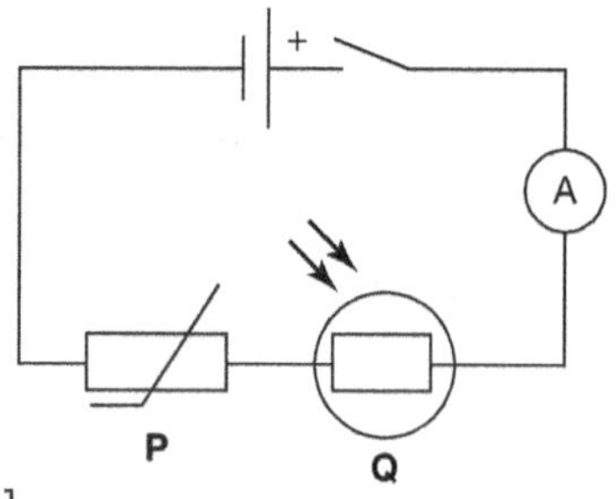

Figure 7

a Identify components **P** and **Q**.

P: _____   Q: _____   [2 marks]

b Describe a change affecting component **P** that would cause the ammeter reading to increase.

_____

_____ [1 mark]

c Describe a change affecting component **Q** that would cause the ammeter reading to decrease.

_____

_____ [1 mark]

d Which component, **P** or **Q**, would be suitable for use in a circuit designed to control the temperature of a tropical fish tank?

Component: _____   [1 mark]

2. The *I–V* characteristic graph for a circuit component is shown in **Figure 8**.

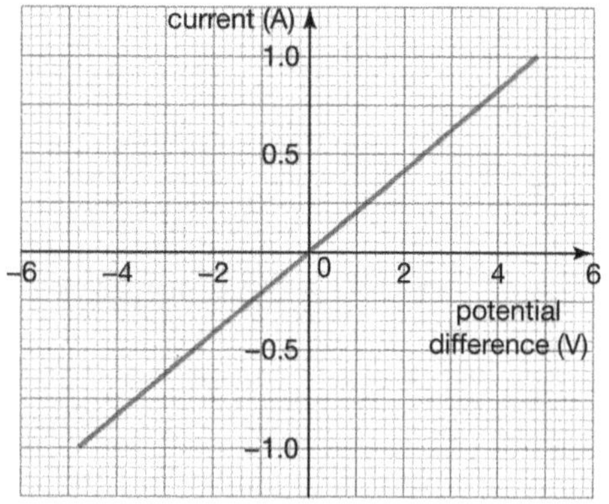

a Which feature of the graph shows that the current through the component is directly proportional to the potential difference across the component?

_____

_____ [1 mark]

Figure 8

b Give **one** property of the component that can be concluded from the graph.

_____ [1 mark]

3. *I–V* characteristic graphs for three components, **A**, **B** and **C**, are shown in **Figure 9**.

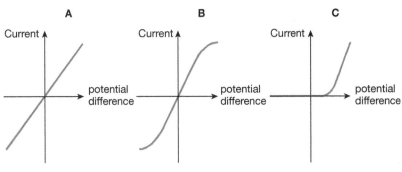

Figure 9

a Which graph represents a diode? Tick **one** box.

A ☐   **B** ☐   **C** ☐   [1 mark]

b Which graph represents a component whose resistance increases as the current through it increases? Tick **one** box.

A ☐   **B** ☐   **C** ☐   [1 mark]

4. A student is asked to investigate how the current through a component changes as the potential difference across the component is changed. The component being investigated is labelled **X** in **Figure 10**.

Required practical

a Draw a circuit diagram in **Figure 10** that the student could use to obtain a range of current and potential difference values.   [3 marks]

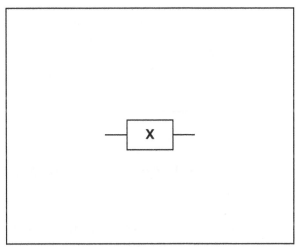

Figure 10

b Describe how the student could obtain current and potential difference data to plot an *I–V* characteristic graph for component X. You should name the apparatus used and include a procedure to reduce random errors.

Literacy

A plan for an investigation should be written so that the steps involved are in a logical sequence that another person could follow and get good results.

_____

_____

_____

_____

_____

_____

_____

_____ [6 marks]

Series and parallel circuits

Worked
Example
Calculate the reading on the ammeter in **Figure 11** when the switch is open and when the switch is closed. [6 marks]

Remember

The combined resistance of two or more components in series is the sum of their resistances.

When the switch is open, the circuit contains a 4.0 Ω resistor and an 8.0 Ω resistor in series.

The total circuit resistance is = 4.0 + 8.0 = 12.0 Ω [1 mark]

Using $V = IR$, 6.0 = I × 12 [1 mark]

Ammeter reading, $I = \frac{6.0}{12}$ [1 mark]

= 0.50 A [1 mark]

Closing the switch short circuits the 4.0 Ω resistor.

This leaves just the 8.0 Ω in the circuit, which gives the new ammeter reading,

$I = \frac{6.0}{8.0}$ [1 mark]

= 0.75 A [1 mark]

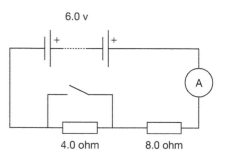

6.0 v

4.0 ohm   8.0 ohm

Figure 11

24

1. Calculate the reading on the ammeter in **Figure 12** when the switch is open and when the switch is closed.

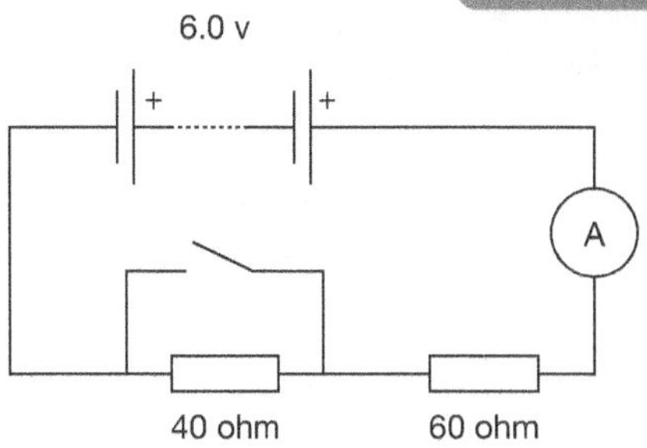

Maths Skills

6.0 v

A

40 ohm   60 ohm

Figure 12

Current reading (switch open) = _____ A

Current reading (switch closed) = _____ A   [6 marks]

2. In **Figure 13**, Component Y has a resistance of $1.4\,k\Omega$.

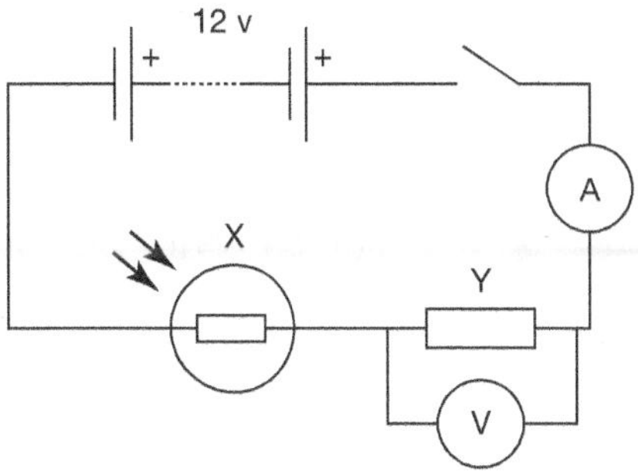

Maths Skills

a In daylight, component X has a resistance of $600\,\Omega$.

Calculate the total resistance in the circuit in daylight.

12 v

A

X

Y

V

Figure 13

Resistance = _____ Ω.   [1 mark]

b Calculate the reading on the ammeter when the circuit is in daylight.

Give your answer in mA

Ammeter reading = _____ m A   [4 marks]

c Calculate the reading on the voltmeter when the circuit is in daylight.

Voltmeter reading = _____ V   [2 marks]

d Component X is now covered so that it is in darkness.

Explain how this will affect the voltmeter reading.

> **Command word**
>
> **Explain** means you have to write what happens and why it happens.

_____

_____

_____   [4 marks]

Figure 14 shows a circuit with three identical 10 Ω resistors connected in parallel.

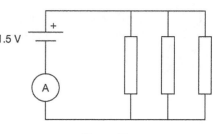

Figure 14

a Determine the potential difference across each resistor. [1 mark]

b Determine the current through each resistor. [3 marks]

c Determine the current drawn from the cell. [1 mark]

a Since the ends of each resistor are connected directly to the cell, the potential difference across each resistor is 1.5 V. [1 mark]

b Using $V = IR$, $1.5 = I \times 10$ [1 mark]

Current through one resistor, $I = \frac{1.5}{10}$ [1 mark]

$= 0.15\,A$ [1 mark]

c The total current is the sum of all currents through each branch. Therefore to supply 0.15 A to each of the three resistors means that the current drawn from the cell must be 0.45 A. [1 mark]

3. Three different resistors are connected to a cell as shown in **Figure 15**.

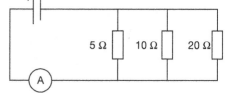

Figure 15

Which statements apply to the circuit in **Figure 15**?

Tick **two** boxes.

The potential difference across each of the resistors has the same value ☐

The potential difference across each of the resistors has a different value ☐

The current through each of the resistors has the same value ☐

The current through each of the resistors has a different value ☐ [2 marks]

4. The resistors in **Figure 16** each have a resistance of 20 Ω.

a Give the potential difference across each resistor.

Potential difference = _____ V [1 mark]

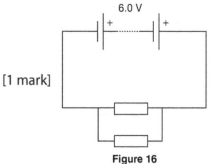

Figure 16

b Calculate the current through one of the resistors.

Current = _____ A   [3 marks]

c Determine the current drawn from the battery.

Current = _____ A   [1 mark]

Mains electricity

1. The mains supplies an alternating potential difference. The potential difference from a battery is a direct supply.

   Explain the difference between an alternating potential difference and a direct potential difference.

   _____

   _____

   _____   [2 marks]

2. What are the correct values for both the mains potential difference and frequency?

   Tick **one** box.

Mains p.d.	Frequency	
230 V	100 Hz	☐
230 V	50 Hz	☐
120 V	50 Hz	☐

   [1 mark]

3. Mains appliances with a metal casing require a cable containing a live wire, a neutral wire and an earth wire.

   a Describe the purpose of the live and the neutral wires.

   The live wire: _____

   _____

   The neutral wire: _____

   _____   [2 marks]

b Explain how the earth wire protects the person using the appliance if the live wire became loose and touched the appliance's metal casing.

_____

_____

_____

_____ [4 marks]

Energy changes in circuits

 Worked Example An electric kettle has a power rating of 2000 W.

Calculate how much energy is transferred from the mains if the kettle is switched on for 5 minutes.

[2 marks]

Remember
You need to learn the equation that links energy transferred by electrical working to power and time as you may not be given the equation in the exam.

Energy transferred = power × time

= 2000 × 5 × 60   [1 mark]

= 600 000 J   [1 mark]

1. An electric lawnmower has a power rating of 1.0 kW. Calculate the energy transferred by the mower if it takes 15 minutes to mow the lawn.

Maths Skills

Energy transferred = _____ J   [3 marks]

2. An electric oven operates at power of 2.0 kW.

Maths Skills Calculate how much energy is transferred if the oven is switched on for 1 hour. Give your answer in standard form.

Maths
Answers given in standard form should only have one digit in front of the decimal point.

Energy = _____ J   [4 marks]

A hand-held fan is connected to a 3.0 V battery. 30 C of charge passes through the motor inside the fan while it is switched on for a period of time.

Calculate the energy transferred by the motor while it is switched on. [2 marks]

Remember

You need to learn the equation that links energy transferred to charge flow and potential difference as you may not be given the equation in the exam.

Energy transferred: $E = QV$

$$= 30 \times 3.0$$ [1 mark]

$$= 90 \text{ J}$$ [1 mark]

3. An electric heater is connected to the 230 V mains supply and switched on for a period of time then switched off.

a Describe the energy transfer that is taking place.

_____ [1 mark]

Maths Skills

b Whilst the heater is switched on, 16 000 C of charge flows through the heater.

Calculate the energy transferred by the heater. Give your answer in standard form to 2 significant figures.

Energy = _____ J [3 marks]

4. An electric toy car, connected to a 3.0 V battery, operates at a power of 2.0 W.

Maths Skills

a Calculate the energy transferred to the toy car to make it move for 15 s.

Energy = _____ J [2 marks]

b Calculate the charge that flows through the motor inside the toy car while it is moving.

Charge = _____ C [3 marks]

Electrical power

 Calculate the electric current drawn from the 230 V mains by a 920 W hairdryer. [3 marks]

Using the equation $P = VI$

$$920 = 230 \times I$$ [1 mark]

$$\text{Current } I = \frac{920}{230}$$ [1 mark]

$$= 4.0 \text{ A}$$ [1 mark]

Maths

You need to learn the equation that links electrical power to potential difference and current as you may not be given the equation in the exam.

1. Calculate the electric current drawn from the 230 V mains supply by a 1.2 kW electric lawnmower. Give your answer to 2 significant figures.

Maths Skills

Current = _____ [5 marks]

2. **a** A 460 W television is connected to the 230 V mains supply. Calculate the current drawn by the TV.

Maths Skills

Current = _____ A [3 marks]

b Calculate the overall electrical resistance of the television.

Resistance = _____ Ω [3 marks]

 A resistor connected to a battery transfers thermal energy to its surroundings when current passes through the resistor.

Calculate the power dissipated by a 1.5 kΩ resistor carrying a current of 2.0 mA. [3 marks]

1.5 kΩ = 1500 Ω and 2.0 mA = 0.0020 A [1 mark]

Maths

You need to learn the equation that links electrical power to current and resistance as you may not be given the equation in the exam.

Power, $P = I^2R$

$$= (0.0020)^2 \times 1500 \qquad \text{[1 mark]}$$

$$= 0.0060\,W \qquad \text{[1 mark]}$$

3. The connecting leads in a series circuit have a total resistance of $0.30\,\Omega$. The leads are carrying a current of $0.20\,A$. Calculate the power dissipated by the leads.

Maths Skills

Power = _____ W   [2 marks]

4. A $4.0\,k\Omega$ resistor in a circuit carries a current of $2.0\,mA$. Calculate the energy transferred by the resistor to the surroundings in 5 minutes.

Maths Skills

Maths

Some high-level multi-step questions may require you to use more than one equation.

Energy = _____ J   [5 marks]

The National Grid

1. **a** The National Grid links power stations at different locations in the UK to consumers all over the country.

Explain why it is better to have your house connected to the National Grid rather than to just one local power station.

_____

_____

_____   [2 marks]

b The National Grid consists of overhead power lines along with step-up and step-down transformers. Describe the difference in the function of a step-up and a step-down transformer.

_____

_____   [1 mark]

2. **a** Calculate the power dissipated to the surroundings by a National Grid cable of resistance $100\,\Omega$ carrying a current of $30\,A$.

Maths Skills

Synoptic
There are more questions on transformers in Section 7.

Power = _____ W   [2 marks]

b At a power station, electricity is generated at a potential difference of 25 kV.

A step-up transformer at the power station increases the 25 kV to 400 kV. This has the effect of reducing the current in the cables.

Explain why it is an advantage to transmit electrical power at a smaller current.

_____

_____

_____   [2 marks]

c Explain why it is necessary to have step-down transformers between the National Grid power lines and factories, schools and houses.

_____

_____   [1 mark]

Static electricity

1. **a** A student finds that when he rubs a polythene rod with a cloth, the rod becomes negatively charged. Explain in terms of electron movement why the polythene rod becomes negatively charged.

_____

_____   [2 marks]

b The student suspends the charged polythene rod as shown in **Figure 17**. As he moves a charged acetate rod towards the polythene rod, the charged polythene rod rotates towards the acetate rod.

Explain this observation.

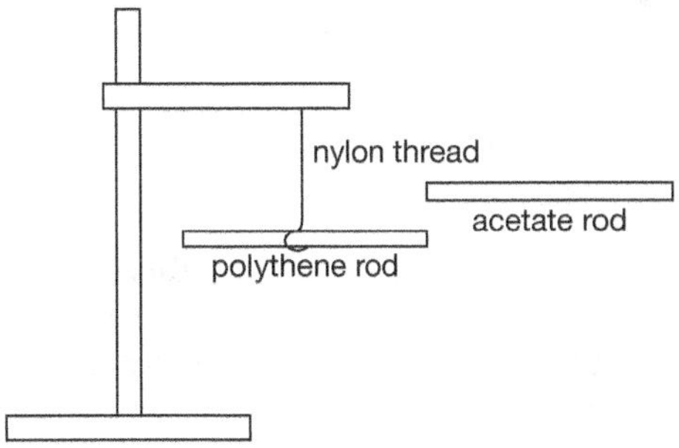

Figure 17

_____

_____ [2 marks]

Electric fields

1. **a** State how you could test to see if an electric field exists in the space around an object.

_____

_____ [1 mark]

b The circle in **Figure 18** represents an isolated sphere with a positive charge.

Draw electric field lines on **Figure 18** to show the electric field created by the sphere. [2 marks]

Figure 18

c **Figure 19** shows two isolated spheres with positive charges.

Describe the force between the spheres as they are pushed closer together.

Figure 19

_____

_____ [2 marks]

Density

1.

Maths Skills

a Mercury metal is poured into a measuring cylinder. The volume of mercury is 4.5 cm³. The mass of mercury in the cylinder is 61.2 g.

Calculate the density of mercury. Give the unit.

Maths

You need to know the equation relating density to mass and volume as you may not be given the equation in the question.

Density = _____ Unit _____   [3 marks]

Maths Skills

b Use your answer to part (a) to find the volume of mercury that has a mass of 54.5 g.

Give your answer to 2 significant figures.

Volume = _____ cm³   [4 marks]

2.

Maths Skills

A swimming pool has dimensions of 25.00 m × 8.50 m and is filled to a depth of 1.20 m. Calculate the mass of water in the pool.

Density of water = 1000 kg/m³.

Mass = _____ kg   [4 marks]

3.

Maths Skills

Find the mass, in grams of 200 cm³ ethanol. Ethanol has a density of 789 kg/m³.

Maths

Density is given in kg/m³ but the volume is given in cm³. You need to work in grams and cm³ all the way through, so change the units of density to g/cm³ before starting the calculation. Alternatively, change the units of volume to m³ before starting the calculation, to give an answer in kg which you then convert to grams.

Mass = _____ g   [4 marks]

4.

Maths Skills

Find the volume of olive oil that has a mass of 255 g.

Density of olive oil = 0.92 g/cm³.

Give your answer in cubic centimetres to 2 significant figures.

Volume = _____ cm³   [4 marks]

5.

Required practical

A student is given the apparatus in **Figure 1** and asked to measure the volume of the pebble.

Describe how the student should make this measurement.

Include in your answer a suitable estimate of the uncertainty in the measurement. Justify your answer.

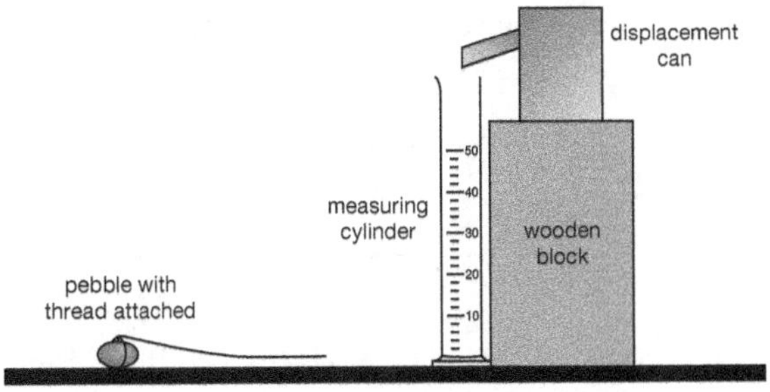

Figure 1

_____

_____

_____

_____

_____

_____ [4 marks]

6.

Maths Skills

The density of seawater near the surface of the ocean is 1030 kg/m³ at 4 °C.

As the ocean temperature increases, the density of seawater decreases.

State what will happen to the volume of the ocean as temperature increases. Give a reason for your answer.

_____

_____ [2 marks]

Changes of state

1.

When heated, iodine does not melt. Instead the solid changes directly into a gas.

a What name is given to this change of state?

_____ [1 mark]

b Explain how you could show this process is a physical (not chemical) change.

_____

_____ [2 marks]

2. A solid substance is heated from room temperature. **Figure 2** shows the heating curve obtained.

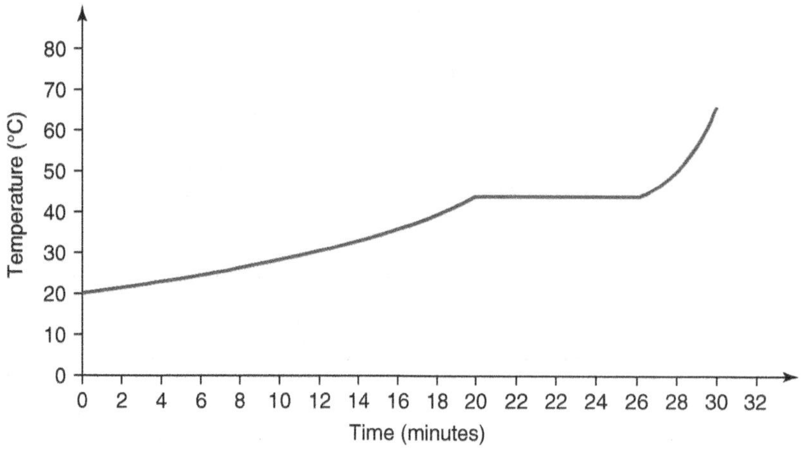

Figure 2

a Use the graph to estimate the melting point of the solid.

Melting point = _____ °C   [1 mark]

b State the freezing point of the solid.

Freezing point = _____ °C   [1 mark]

3. Air is made up of several different gases, which all condense at different temperatures when they are cooled.

Liquid nitrogen at –196 °C is poured over an inflated balloon. The balloon shrinks.

a Give **two** reasons why the volume of the balloon decreases.

1 _____

2 _____ [2 marks]

b State what will happen to the mass of the balloon and its contents.

_____ [1 mark]

c Explain your answer to part (b).

_____

_____ [2 marks]

Internal energy and specific latent heat

1. A balloon contains nitrogen gas at room temperature.

a Give the term that describes the total kinetic energy and potential energy of the gas particles in the balloon.

_____ [1 mark]

The balloon is cooled by pouring over liquid nitrogen, which is −196 °C. Some of the nitrogen gas in the balloon cools to −196°C and then condenses.

b State what happens to the kinetic energy of nitrogen gas particles at −196°C as the gas condenses.

Give a reason for your answer.

_____

_____ [2 marks]

2. Calculate the energy transferred to 20 g of water to change it from the liquid state to the gaseous state.

Maths Skills

The specific latent heat of vaporisation of water is 2.26 MJ/kg.

Use the correct equation from the Physics equations sheet.

Maths

The equation: $\Delta E = mL$ is provided in the Physics equations sheet. You should be able to select and apply the equation.

Energy transferred = _____ J   [3 marks]

Remember

'mega' is a prefix which is equal to 1 000 000 or 1×10^6. So 1 MJ = 10^6 J.

3. An ice cube with a mass of 10 g sits in a bowl at room temperature. The ice changes from a solid to a liquid while its temperature remains constant.

Maths Skills

Calculate the internal energy change of the ice.

Specific latent heat of fusion for water = 3.34×10^5 J/kg.

Specific latent heat of vaporisation for water = 2.26×10^6 J/kg.

Use the correct equation from the Physics equations sheet.

Internal energy change = _____ J   [3 marks]

4. A block of ice requires 12 000 J to melt completely at its melting point.

Specific latent heat of fusion for ice = 3.34×10^5 J/kg.

Find the mass of water that will be produced.

Give your answer to 2 significant figures.

Maths

In this example you need to rearrange the equation to find the mass, m. When you rearrange an equation, always do the same operation to both sides of the equation. To make m the subject of the equation, divide both sides of the equation by L.

Mass = _____ kg   [4 marks]

Worked Example ▶ A block of ice breaks away from a glacier and falls into the sea. The ice is approximately rectangular with dimensions 125 m × 104 m × 30 m.

Density of ice = 917 kg/m³

Specific latent heat of fusion for ice = 3.34×10^5 J/kg.

Calculate the energy that must be transferred to the iceberg to melt it.   [6 marks]

Problem solving

In 5- or 6-mark calculation questions, you usually have to use different equations from different topics. Write down your working for each part of the problem. By showing correct working you will get some marks even if your final answer is wrong.

Volume of iceberg = 125 × 104 × 30 = 390 000 m³   [1 mark]

$917 = \dfrac{\text{mass of iceberg}}{390\,000}$ [1 mark]

mass = 917 × 390 000   [1 mark]

     = 357 630 000 kg   [1 mark]

To change the state of the ice:

$E = mL$

     = 357 630 000 × 334 000   [1 mark]

     = 1.19×10^{14} J   [1 mark]

5. 0.25 kg water is heated from 20 °C to steam at 100 °C.

Maths Skills

Specific heat capacity of water = 4200 J/kg °C

Specific latent heat of vaporisation of water = 2.26×10^6 J/kg

Synoptic

Calculate the total energy that must be transferred to raise the temperature of the water from 20 °C to 100 °C.

Energy transferred = _____ J   [5 marks]

Particle motion in gases

1. **a** Explain how the air inside a bicycle tyre exerts pressure on the inside wall of the tyre.

_____

_____   [2 marks]

b The temperature of the air inside a bicycle tyre increases during a journey.

Describe what will happen to the pressure in the tyre. Explain your answer.

_____

_____

_____   [3 marks]

2. A scientist collects a sample of gas in a sealed container.

a Describe the movement of the molecules of gas in the container.

_____

_____

_____   [3 marks]

b The container is heated.

State what happens to the average kinetic energy of the molecules of gas in the container.

_____ [1 mark]

Increasing the pressure of a gas

1. The equation linking the pressure of a gas to its volume is

pressure × volume = constant

In order for this equation to be true, which **two** other variables must be kept constant?

_____

_____ [2 marks]

Maths

The equation relating pressure to volume is provided in the Physics equations sheet. You should be able to select and apply the equation.

The pump used to inflate a bicycle tyre contains air with a volume of $50\,cm^3$. Initially the air has a pressure of $100\,kPa$. The air is compressed slowly by pushing the handle in.

Calculate the new pressure of the air on the walls of the pump when the volume of trapped air is $10\,cm^3$. The temperature of the compressed air stays constant.

Use the correct equation from the Physics equations sheet. [4 marks]

Maths

The equation is given in the form $pV =$ constant in the Physics equations sheet. But remembering the version: $p_1V_1 = p_2V_2$ may be more helpful. The subscript '1' refers to 'initial' and '2' to 'final'.

$pV =$ constant

$\quad = 100 \times 50 = 5000$ [1 mark]

$p_2 \times 10 = 5000$ [1 mark]

The new pressure, $p_2 = \frac{5000}{10}$ [1 mark]

$\quad = 500\,kPa$ [1 mark]

Maths

You can use units of kPa and cm^3 in this equation as long as you remember that the same units should also be used for the new pressure and the new volume.

2.

Maths Skills

An inflated helium balloon contains helium at a pressure of 120 kPa. The volume of the balloon is 5.0×10^{-3} m³.

The balloon is released from ground level. As the air pressure outside the balloon decreases, the gas pressure inside the balloon decreases because the balloon expands. The temperature does not change.

Find the volume of the balloon at an altitude where the gas pressure inside the balloon is 75 kPa.

Use the correct equation from the Physics equations sheet.

Volume = _____ m³   [4 marks]

3.

Higher Tier only

When air in a bicycle pump is rapidly compressed by moving the pump quickly in and out, the air inside the pump gets hot.

Explain why the temperature of the air inside the pump increases.

_____

_____

_____   [3 marks]

Protons, neutrons and electrons

1. Describe how the electrons are arranged in an atom that has several electrons.

_____

_____ [2 marks]

2. **a** Name the **two** particles that make up most of the mass of an atom.

1 _____

2 _____ [2 marks]

b State where these particles are located in the atom.

_____ [1 mark]

3. State what happens when electrons in an atom move to a lower energy level.

_____ [1 mark]

4. Describe what causes electrons in an atom to move to a higher energy level.

_____ [1 mark]

5. State whether electrons in a higher energy level are closer to, or further from the nucleus.

_____ [1 mark]

The size of atoms

Write 0.000 000 000 001 m in standard form. [1 mark]

First, place the decimal point after the first non-zero
digit. Then work out how many places this has moved the
digit. This is the negative power of 10.

0.000 000 000 001 m = 1.0×10^{-12} m

Maths

Answers given in standard
form should have only
one digit in front of the
decimal point.

[1 mark]

42

1. The approximate size of the radius of an atom is 0.1 nm.

Maths
Skills
Write this value in metres, using standard form.

Radius = _____ m [1 mark]

Maths

Remember that the more negative the power of 10, the smaller the number. So 10^{-4} m is 10 times smaller than 10^{-3} m.

2. **a** State the approximate ratio of the size of an atom to the size of the nucleus.

_____ [1 mark]

Maths
Skills
b By how many orders of magnitude is an atom bigger than the nucleus?

_____ [1 mark]

c Write the approximate size of the nucleus in metres, using standard form.

_____ [1 mark]

Maths

Orders of magnitude can be used to make approximate comparisons. If two values differ by two orders of magnitude, then one value is approximately 10^2 (or 100) times bigger than the other.

3. The radius of a gold atom is 0.270 nm.

Maths
Skills
a Write this value in metres using standard form.

Radius = _____ m [1 mark]

4. The radius of a lithium atom is 0.152 nm.

Maths
Skills
a Write this value in metres using standard form.

Radius = _____ m [1 mark]

b The equation for the volume of a sphere, V is $V = \frac{4}{3}\pi r^3$ where r is the radius.

Use the equation to estimate the volume of a lithium atom.

Give your answer to 2 significant figures in standard form.

Volume of a lithium atom = _____ m^3 [3 marks]

5. The helium atom has a radius of 1.2×10^{-10} m and its nucleus a radius of 1.9×10^{-15} m.

Calculate how many times larger the atom is compared to the nucleus.

Give your answer to 2 significant figures.

Number of times larger = _____   [3 marks]

Elements and isotopes

1. An atom of the isotope helium-4 can be represented by the symbol $_2^4 He$.

Use this information to draw a representation of an atom of this isotope.

[3 marks]

2. **Table 1** shows data for six different nuclei.

Nucleus	Atomic number	Mass number	Number of neutrons
A	88	226	
B		224	136
C	85		141
D	86	224	
E		222	136
F		226	134

Table 1

a   Complete the missing values in **Table 1**.   [6 marks]

b   Give the letters of **two** pairs of isotopes of the same element.

_____   [2 marks]

3. The symbol for the nucleus of one of the isotopes of polonium is $^{210}_{84}$Po.

Command words

When the question says **determine** you must use the data you are given to calculate an answer.

a Determine the numbers of the different subatomic particles present in a polonium nucleus.

_____

_____ [2 marks]

b A different isotope of polonium has 134 neutrons in its nucleus.

Add the atomic number and mass number to the symbol for this isotope. [2 marks]

———Po

Electrons and ions

1. An atom of carbon-14 loses an electron to form an ion.

a State the charge on the ion.

_____ [1 mark]

b The atomic number of carbon is 6. Determine the numbers of protons, neutrons and electrons in the ion.

Number of protons = _____

Number of neutrons = _____

Number of electrons = _____ [3 marks]

2. An atom of oxygen gains two electrons to form an ion.

The atomic number of oxygen is 8 and the mass number of this atom is 16. Determine the numbers of protons, neutrons and electrons in the ion.

Number of protons = _____

Number of neutrons = _____

Number of electrons = _____ [3 marks]

3. An atom of magnesium loses two electrons to form an ion.

The atomic number of magnesium is 12 and the mass number of this atom is 24. Determine the numbers of protons, neutrons and electrons in the ion.

Number of protons = _____

Number of neutrons = _____

Number of electrons = _____   [3 marks]

Discovering the structure of the atom

1. From 1908 to 1909, scientists carried out experiments in which they fired alpha particles at a very thin sheet of gold foil.

a Describe the results obtained from this experiment.

_____

_____

_____   [2 marks]

b Explain how these results led to the plum pudding model of the atom being replaced.

_____

_____

_____

Remember

When answering 6-mark extended writing questions you will get a mark in one of three bands based on the overall quality of your answer (how logically it is structured and how coherent it is). The mark within the band depends on the standard of the scientific response.

_____

_____

_____

_____   [6 marks]

2. Describe how the nuclear model of the atom was adjusted by Niels Bohr.

_____

_____

_____ [2 marks]

Radioactive decay

1. What is recorded by a Geiger–Muller tube? Tick **one** box.

The number of alpha or beta particles emitted ☐

The number of radioactive decays per second ☐

The time it takes for the count rate to drop to half its starting level ☐ [1 mark]

2. Iodine-131 decays by emitting both beta and gamma radiation. Describe the nature of these types of radiation.

_____

_____ [2 marks]

3. Describe how beta particles are emitted from an atom of a radioactive isotope.

_____

_____

_____ [2 marks]

4. Describe how alpha particles are emitted from an atom of a radioactive isotope.

_____

_____

_____ [2 marks]

5. How can the count rate of a radioactive source be measured? Tick **one** box.

Record count rate and subtract the background count rate. ☐

Measure the thickness of absorber needed to reduce the count rate to zero. ☐

Measure the time it takes for the count rate to drop to half its starting level. ☐ [1 mark]

Comparing alpha, beta and gamma radiation

1. Complete **Table 2** to compare the properties of alpha, beta and gamma radiation. [6 marks]

Radiation type	Approximate range in air	Ionising power (high/medium/low)
alpha		
beta		
gamma		

Table 2

2. Radioactive isotopes can be injected into a person as a medical tracer. The radiation emitted by the tracer is then detected outside the patient's body.

Explain why a radioactive isotope that emits alpha radiation would never be used as a medical tracer.

_____

_____

_____ [2 marks]

3. Leaks in a buried pipe can be detected by injecting a radioactive isotope into the flow of water in the pipe. When water leaks out into the soil, the tracer also leaks out. The increased level of radioactivity above ground is detected using a Geiger–Muller tube.

Table 3 gives information about five radioactive isotopes.

Isotope	Half-life	Radiation emitted
americium-241	432 years	alpha
cobalt-60	5.3 years	gamma
iodine-131	8 days	beta and gamma
phosphorus-32	14 days	beta
sodium-24	15 hours	beta and gamma

Table 3

Determine which radioactive isotope would be most suitable for detecting leaks from a buried pipe. Use your knowledge and the information from the table.

_____

_____

_____

_____

_____

_____ [4 marks]

Radioactive decay equations

1. Carbon-14 decays by emitting a beta particle.

Complete the nuclear equation to show the beta decay of carbon into nitrogen.

$$^{14}_{}C \rightarrow\ ^{}_{7}N +\ ^{0}_{-1}e$$ [2 marks]

2. An atom of uranium-235 decays to form an atom of thorium-231 by emitting radiation.

$$^{235}_{92}U \rightarrow {}^{231}_{90}Th + radiation$$

What type of radiation, alpha, beta or gamma, is emitted by uranium-235?

Give a reason for your answer.

_____

_____

_____ [2 marks]

3. Radium-226 is a radioactive isotope that decays to an isotope of radon (Rn) by alpha decay.

Complete the nuclear equation to show the alpha decay of radium-226.

$$^{226}_{\underline{}}Ra \rightarrow {}^{\overline{}}_{86}Rn + \underline{}\underline{}\,\underline{}$$ [3 marks]

4. Polonium-210 is a radioactive isotope that decays to an isotope of lead (Pb) by alpha decay.

Complete the nuclear equation to show the alpha decay of polonium-210.

$$^{210}_{\underline{}}Po \rightarrow {}^{\overline{}}_{82}Pb + \underline{}\underline{}\,\underline{}$$ [3 marks]

Half-lives

Radium-226 has a half-life of 1600 years.

A sample of rock containing radium-226 has a count rate of 600 counts per second.

Determine how long it will it take for the count rate to reduce to approximately 75 counts per second.
[2 marks]

$600 \rightarrow 300 \rightarrow 150 \rightarrow 75$

We have halved 600, then halved 300, then halved 150. This is 3 half-lives.
[1 mark]

Time taken = 3 x 1600 years = 4800 years
[1 mark]

Common misconception
The count rate will not be exactly 75 after three half-lives because radioactivity is a **random** process and the time for the activity to halve may not be exactly the same each time.

1. A radioactive source has a half-life of 20 minutes.

Maths Skills

At 10:00, the source's activity is 70 kBq. Predict the source's activity at 11:40.

Give your answer in Bequerel (Bq).

Activity = _____ Bq   [3 marks]

2. The half-life of fermium-253 is 3 days.

a If a source has an activity of 280 Bq, what will its activity be after 12 days?

Activity = _____ Bq   [3 marks]

b A sample is estimated to contain 5.0×10^6 fermium-253 nuclei. Calculate how long it will take until approximately 40 000 fermium-253 nuclei remain.

Time taken = _____ minutes   [3 marks]

3. **a** The activity of a radioactive source is recorded every hour. After 24 hours, the activity has decreased from 128 Bq to 2 Bq. What is the half-life of the isotope?

Half-life = _____ hours   [3 marks]

b Calculate the fraction of the original isotope remaining after 24 hours.

Fraction remaining = _____   [1 mark]

4. The graph in **Figure 1** shows how the activity of a sample of protactinium-234 changes with time.

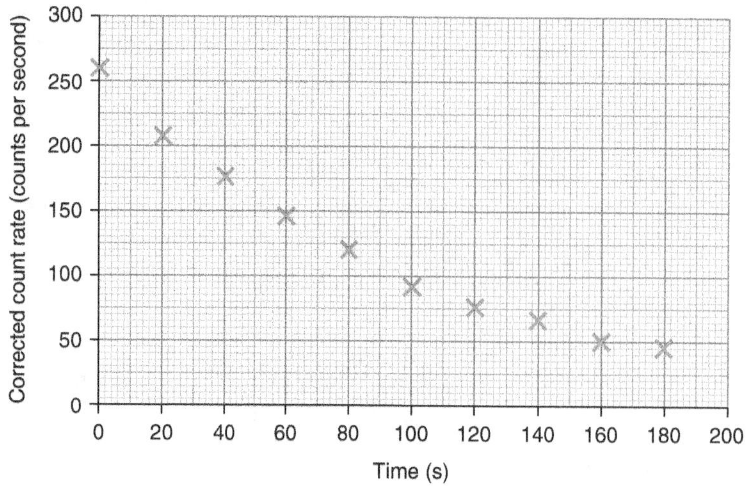

Figure 1

The data have been corrected for the background count.

a Draw a line of best fit on the graph. [1 mark]

b Use the graph to determine the half-life of protactinium-234. Show clearly on the graph how you obtained this value.

Half-life value = _____ s [3 marks]

Worked Example

Calculate the net decline in the activity of a sample of a radioactive isotope after three half-lives. [2 marks]

Higher Tier only

Three half-lives: $1 \rightarrow \frac{1}{2} \rightarrow \frac{1}{4} \rightarrow \frac{1}{8}$ [1 mark]

net decline = $\dfrac{\text{final number}}{\text{initial number}} = \dfrac{\frac{1}{8}}{1} = \dfrac{1}{8}$ [1 mark]

5. The initial activity of a sample is 6 kBq. After four half-lives the activity has fallen to 375 Bq. Calculate the net decline in the activity of the sample, expressed as a ratio, after four half-lives.

Net decline = _____ [2 marks]

Radioactive contamination

1. Describe **two** ways of preventing exposure to irradiation from radioactive materials.

_____

_____ [2 marks]

2. Explain why contamination by an alpha emitter may cause a greater hazard than contamination by a gamma emitter.

_____

_____ [2 marks]

3. Suggest **two** ways a person working at a hospital could become contaminated by radioactive materials.

_____

_____ [2 marks]

4. Compare irradiation and radioactive contamination.

Include in your answer a comparison of the hazards associated with contamination and irradiation.

Command words

A **compare** question means describe both similarities and differences.

_____

_____

_____

_____

_____ [4 marks]

Background radiation

1. Give **one** natural source of background radiation.

_____ [1 mark]

2. Radiation dose is measured in sieverts (Sv). Some typical radiation doses are given in **Table 4**.

Exposure to background radiation	Radiation dose (mSv)
Average UK annual dose	2.7
Annual dose for residents of Cornwall	7.8
CT scan of abdomen/pelvis	10
Residents near Sellafield, from eating locally caught lobster / crab	0.41
Worker at nuclear power station	0.18
Recreational user of beaches in north Cumbria	0.01
Typical flight from the UK to Spain	0.01
Eating 1 banana	0.01

Table 4

a Write 10 mSv in Sv.

_____ [1 mark]

b Sellafield, on the Cumbrian coast, is a former nuclear power station that is being decommissioned. The site also stores nearly all the radioactive waste generated by the UK's nuclear reactors. Monitoring of beaches near Sellafield for radioactive contamination has found small numbers of radioactive objects the size of grains of sand, or small slivers of radioactive plastic or metal.

Give **two** reasons the individual dose of background radiation for a resident of Cumbria may be higher than the UK average due to their occupation.

_____

_____ [2 marks]

c The current advice from Public Health England and the Food Standards Agency is that the overall health risk from radioactive particles for beach users in Cumbria is very low.

Command words

Justify means to use evidence from the information supplied to support an answer. Here, you are asked about the risks to beach users in Cumbria so you should list some reasons for being concerned or not concerned and evaluate how well the data supports the statement.

Use your knowledge and the information from the table to justify this statement.

_____

_____

_____

_____

_____

_____

_____

_____

_____

_____

_____ [6 marks]

Uses and hazards of nuclear radiation

1. Nuclear radiation can be used to kill cancer cells. State why this treatment may also harm a patient.

_____ [1 mark]

2. **Table 5** gives data on two radioactive isotopes used in medical imaging and treatment.

Table 5

Isotope	Half-life	Radiation emitted
radium-223	11.4 days	alpha
technetium-99m	6 hours	gamma

a Use the data to explain why technetium-99m is suitable for use as a tracer for producing images of internal organs.

_____

_____

_____ [2 marks]

b Use the data to explain why radium-223 is more suitable for putting inside the body to treat cancerous tumours than for use as a tracer.

_____

_____

_____ [2 marks]

c Hospital staff caring for patients receiving treatment with radium-223 are advised to wash their hands with soap and water after patient contact rather than using hand sanitiser. Explain why.

_____

_____

_____ [2 marks]

3. **Table 6** gives data on some radioactive isotopes present in radioactive waste from nuclear power stations.

Table 6

Isotope	Half-life (years)
caesium-137	30
plutonium-239	2.4×10^3
strontium-90	29
uranium-235	7.0×10^8
uranium-238	4.5×10^9

Describe, using the information from **Table 6**, how the hazard from waste containing these radioactive materials will change with time.

_____

_____

_____

_____ [4 marks]

Nuclear fission

1.   **a**   Nuclear power stations rely on the fission of uranium-235.

       State what must happen for fission of uranium-235 to occur.

       _____ [2 marks]

   b   Describe what happens to the nucleus of an atom during nuclear fission.

       _____

       _____

       _____ [3 marks]

2.   Plutonium-239 can be used to make a nuclear fission bomb.

   a   Explain how the fission of plutonium-239 can lead to a chain reaction.

       _____

       _____

       _____

       _____ [4 marks]

b Describe **one** difference between a chain reaction in a nuclear bomb and in a nuclear reactor.

_____ [1 mark]

Nuclear fusion

1. Describe what happens to the nuclei of atoms during nuclear fusion.

_____

_____ [2 marks]

2. An experimental nuclear fusion reactor has succeeded in releasing energy from the fusion of two isotopes of hydrogen, deuterium and tritium.

Synoptic

The nucleus of the isotope deuterium can be represented by the symbol ^2_1H.

The nucleus of the isotope tritium can be represented by the symbol ^3_1H.

a State the difference between the isotopes deuterium and tritium.

_____ [1 mark]

b The overall effect of the fusion reaction is to convert one deuterium nucleus and one tritium nucleus into one helium nucleus and a neutron.

Complete the nuclear equation to show the fusion of deuterium and tritium.

$$^3_1H + {}^2_1H \rightarrow \underline{}He + {}^1_0n$$ [2 marks]

c In this reaction the mass of the products (a helium nucleus and a neutron) is less than the mass of the deuterium nucleus and tritium nucleus added together.

State what happens to the mass lost from the two hydrogen nuclei.

_____ [1 mark]

Scalars and vectors

1. **a** Explain the difference between a scalar and a vector quantity.

    _____

    _____ [2 marks]

    b Give an example of a scalar quantity.

    _____ [1 mark]

    c Give an example of a vector quantity.

    _____ [1 mark]

2. **Figure 1** shows the route taken by a cyclist travelling from village A to village B.

    Maths Skills Use the diagram to determine the cyclist's displacement. Show how you obtain your answer.

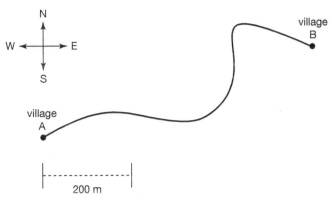

Figure 1

Distance = _____ m

Direction _____ [2 marks]

Speed and velocity

 Worked Example
A driver travels 108 km in 2 hours. Calculate the car's average speed in km/h and in m/s. [5 marks]

Distance travelled, $s = vt$

$$108 = v \times 2 \qquad \text{[1 mark]}$$

which rearanges to give average speed,
$$v = \frac{108}{2} \qquad \text{[1 mark]}$$

$$= 54 \text{ km/h} \qquad \text{[1 mark]}$$

Speed in m/s $= 54 \times 1000 \div 3600$ [1 mark]

$$= 15 \text{ m/s} \qquad \text{[1 mark]}$$

Maths

You need to learn the equation: $s = vt$ where s is distance, v is speed and t is time, as it may not be given to you in the question.

Answer checking

It is useful to know these typical speed estimates so you can check that your answers to velocity calculations are realistic: walking 1.5 m/s; jogging 3 m/s; cycling 6 m/s; car 20 m/s; aircraft 200 m/s.

1.

Maths Skills

An aircraft travels 60 km in a straight line due East. The journey takes 240 s. Calculate the aircraft's average speed in m/s and km/h.

Average speed = _____ m/s

Average speed = _____ km/h [4 marks]

2.

Maths Skills

What would be a suitable estimate for how long it would take to jog 4 km?

Tick **one** box.

120 s ☐   360 s ☐   1200 s ☐   3000 s ☐ [1 mark]

3.

Maths Skills

The distance–time graphs for three different car journeys are shown in **Figure 2**.

Remember

The gradient of a distance–time graph gives speed. If the slope is changing, the speed is changing.

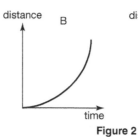
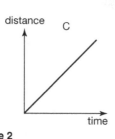
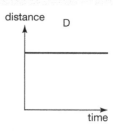

Figure 2

a In which journey does the car have a constant speed?

Tick **one** box.

A ☐   B ☐   C ☐   D ☐   [1 mark]

b In which journey is the car slowing down?

Tick **one** box.

A ☐   B ☐   C ☐   D ☐   [1 mark]

c In which journey is the car speeding up?

Tick **one** box.

A ☐   B ☐   C ☐   D ☐   [1 mark]

4. The first 10 s of a cyclist's journey is shown on the distance–time graph in **Figure 3.**

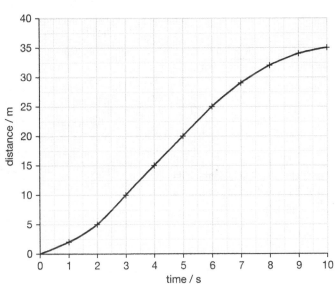

Figure 3

a Between 2 s and 6 s the cyclist has a constant speed. Use **Figure 3** to determine the speed of the cyclist between 2 s and 6 s.

Speed = _____ m/s   [2 marks]

b Between 6 s and 10 s, the cyclist is slowing down.
Use **Figure 3** to determine the cyclist's speed at 8 s.
Show how you obtain your answer.

Speed = _____ m/s   [2 marks]

Remember

For an object that has a speed
that is changing, the speed at a
specific time can be determined
from the distance–time graph by
finding the gradient of a tangent
drawn to the line at that time.

Acceleration

Worked Example

An athlete running at a constant velocity of 5.0 m/s
accelerates for 5.0 s until he reaches a velocity of 6.5 m/s.
Calculate the athlete's acceleration.   [2 marks]

$$\text{Acceleration} = \frac{\text{change in velocity}}{\text{time}}$$

$$= \frac{\text{final velocity} - \text{start velocity}}{\text{time}}$$

$$= \frac{6.5 - 5.0}{5.0} \qquad \text{[1 mark]}$$

$$= 0.30 \text{ m/s}^2 \qquad \text{[1 mark]}$$

Maths

You need to know the
equation that relates
acceleration to change in
velocity and time as it may
not be given to you in the
question.

Maths

The units of acceleration are
m/s^2. Note that the squared
bit only applies to the unit,
not the actual value of the
acceleration.

1.

Maths Skills

A cyclist is travelling along a straight road with a velocity of
6.6 m/s. She then accelerates for 2.0 s reaching a velocity of
7.8 m/s. Calculate the cyclist's acceleration.

Acceleration = _____ m/s^2 [2 marks]

2.

Maths Skills

A car is travelling along a straight road with a velocity of 36 km/h. The car then accelerates for
2.0 s reaching a velocity of 54 km/h. Calculate the car's acceleration.

Acceleration = _____ m/s^2 [3 marks]

3.

Maths Skills

A Formula One car is moving on a straight section of track at a velocity of 10 m/s. The car then
accelerates for 2.0 s with an acceleration of 10 m/s^2.

Calculate the velocity reached by the car after 2.0 s of acceleration.

Velocity = _____ m/s   [3 marks]

4. A velocity–time graph for a moving vehicle is shown in **Figure 4**.

Maths
Skills

Remember

You need to know that the gradient of a velocity–time graph gives the acceleration.

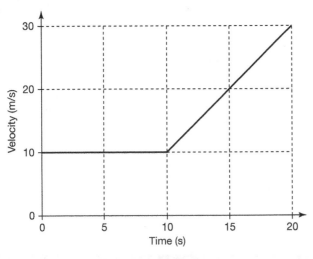

Figure 4

a Use **Figure 4** to determine the time interval during which the vehicle is moving with a constant velocity.

From time = _____ s to time = _____ s   [1 mark]

b Use **Figure 4** to determine the time interval during which the vehicle is accelerating.

From time = _____ s to time = _____ s   [1 mark]

c Use **Figure 4** to determine the acceleration of the vehicle during this time.

Acceleration = _____ m/s²   [2 marks]

Higher Tier only

d Determine the total distance travelled by the vehicle during the 20 s of motion shown in **Figure 4**.

Maths

You need to know that the area enclosed between the line and the time axis of a velocity–time graph gives the distance travelled.

Distance = _____ m   [2 marks]

e Calculate the average speed of the vehicle during the 20 s of motion shown in **Figure 4**. Give your answer in km/h.

Average speed = _____ km/h   [4 marks]

5.

Figure 5 is a velocity–time graph for a skydiver from the moment he jumps out of the aircraft until his parachute opens.

Determine the skydiver's acceleration 15 s after jumping from the aircraft.

Show clearly how you work out your answer.

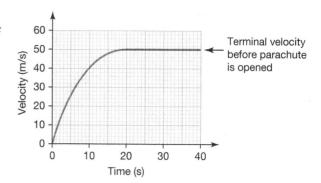

Figure 5

Acceleration = _____ m/s²   [3 marks]

Equation for uniform acceleration

Worked Example

A tram is moving on a straight section of track with a velocity of 5.0 m/s. The tram then accelerates over a distance of 40 m with an acceleration of 0.30 m/s².

Calculate the velocity that the tram reaches after the period of acceleration.   [2 marks]

Initial velocity, $u = 5$ m/s

Distance, $s = 40$ m

Acceleration, $a = 0.30$ m/s²

use $v^2 - u^2 = 2as$

$v^2 - 5^2 = 2 \times 0.30 \times 40$ [1 mark]

$v^2 = 5^2 + (2 \times 0.30 \times 40)$ [1 mark]

$v^2 = 49$, which gives $v = \sqrt{49} = 7.0$ m/s   [1 mark]

Maths

The equation $v^2 - u^2 = 2as$ is on the Physics equations sheet. You are expected to select and apply this equation, but it can only be applied to uniform acceleration.

1.

A cyclist is travelling on a straight section of road with a velocity of 4.0 m/s. She then accelerates over a distance of 40 m with an acceleration of 0.25 m/s².

Calculate the velocity she reaches after the period of acceleration. Use the correct equation from the Physics equations sheet.

Velocity = _____ m/s   [3 marks]

2. An object is dropped from the top of a building of height 50 m. Calculate the speed at which the object would hit the ground. Assume that the object is not affected by air resistance. Use the correct equation from the Physics equations sheet.

Maths Skills

Give your answer to 2 significant figures.

Acceleration due to gravity = 9.8 m/s²

Velocity = _____ m/s   [3 marks]

3. A train accelerates from rest over a distance of 100 m reaching a speed of 10 m/s. Calculate the train's acceleration. Use the correct equation from the Physics equations sheet.

Maths Skills

Acceleration = _____ m/s²   [3 marks]

Forces

Figure 6 shows a box at rest on the ground. On **Figure 6** draw two arrows to show the forces on the box. Label each arrow with the name of the force.   [2 marks]

1 mark given for each correctly labelled arrow.

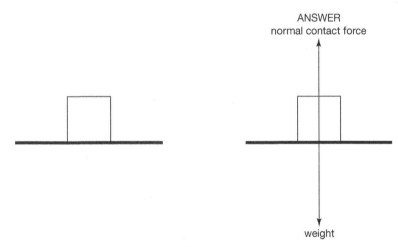

Figure 6

1. **a** **Figure 8** shows a stationary van. On the figure, draw arrows to show forces on the van. Label each arrow with the name of the force.

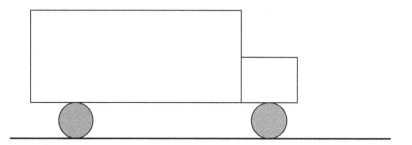

Figure 8

[3 marks]

b Name 3 additional forces that would act on the van if it was moving.

_____

_____

_____ [3 marks]

Moment of a force

 Figure 9 shows a metre rule pivoted at its 50 cm mark. A 2.0 N weight is positioned at the 25 cm mark on the rule. The rule is balanced when the unknown weight, X, is positioned at the 90 cm mark.

a Calculate the moment exerted by the 2.0 N weight about the pivot. Give your answer in N m. [2 marks]

b Calculate the weight of **X**. [3 marks]

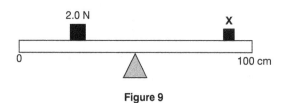

Figure 9

Maths

You need to know the equation that links the moment to the size of the force and the perpendicular distance from the line of action of the force to the pivot as the equation may not be given to you in the question.

Remember

If an object is balanced, the total clockwise moment about the pivot is equal to the total anticlockwise moment about that pivot.

a Moment (anticlockwise) = Fd = 2.0 × (0.50 − 0.25) [1 mark]

= 0.50 N m [1 mark]

b Anticlockwise moment = clockwise moment

$$0.50 = X \times (0.90 - 0.50)$$ [1 mark]

$$\text{Gives } X = \frac{0.50}{0.40}$$ [1 mark]

$$= 1.25\,N$$ [1 mark]

1.

Maths Skills

Figure 10 shows a balanced metre rule pivoted at its centre. The 1.0 N weight is positioned at the 30 cm mark on the metre rule.

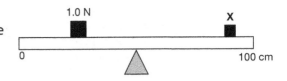

Figure 10

a Calculate the moment exerted by the 1.0 N weight about the pivot.

Give your answer in N m.

Moment = _____ N m [2 marks]

b An unknown weight **X** is positioned at the 85 cm mark. The rule is balanced. Calculate the weight of X. Give your answer to 2 significant figures.

Weight of X = _____ N [4 marks]

2.

Maths Skills

A metre rule is pivoted on a clamped nail through a hole in its centre. The rule supports two weights and is balanced horizontally as shown in **Figure 11**. The 1.0 N weight is positioned 30 cm from the pivot.

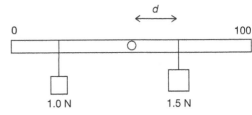

Figure 11

a Calculate the moment exerted by the 1.0 N weight about the pivot.

Give your answer in N m.

Moment = _____ N m [2 marks]

b Calculate the distance, *d*, from the pivot of the 1.5 N weight.

Distance = _____ m [2 marks]

Levers and gears

1.

Maths Skills

A gardener can use a plank of wood as a lever to increase the force that he can exert to enable him to lift a heavy boulder (**Figure 12**).

a The boulder has a weight of 1.00 kN. Calculate the moment that would be required to just lift the boulder off the ground. Give your answer in N m.

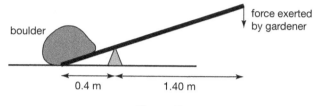

boulder

force exerted by gardener

0.4 m   1.40 m

Figure 12

Moment = _____ N m   [2 marks]

b Calculate the downward force that the gardener would have to apply to the end of the plank to just raise the boulder off the ground.

Give your answer to 3 significant figures.

Force = _____ N   [4 marks]

c The biggest force that the gardener can exert on the end of the plank is 300 N. Calculate the maximum weight he can lift using the lever set up as in **Figure 12**.

Give your answer in kN.

Force = _____ kN   [4 marks]

2. Bicycle gears linked by a chain transmit the rotational effect of the force produced by the cyclist to the back wheel of the bicycle. The chainring attached to the pedals is the larger gear. The rear sprocket at the centre of the back wheel is the smaller gear (**Figure 13**).

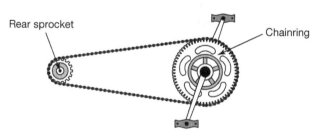

Rear sprocket

Chainring

Figure 13

In **Figure 13** there are 54 teeth on the chainring and 12 on the rear sprocket. Calculate the number of times the rear sprocket rotates for every complete rotation of the chainring.

Number of rotations = _____ N   [1 mark]

Pressure in a fluid

1.

Maths
Skills

The milk in a glass milk bottle has a weight of 5.5 N. The area of the base of the bottle is 0.0038 m².

Calculate the pressure exerted by the milk on the base of the bottle. Give your answer in kPa to 2 significant figures.

Maths

You need to know the equation that relates pressure on a surface to force normal to the surface and area of the surface as you may not be given this equation in the question.

Pressure = _____ kPa   [4 marks]

2.

a A scuba diver is 40 m below the surface of the sea. Calculate the pressure on the diver due to the sea water. Select the correct equation from the Physics equations sheet.

Maths
Skills

Higher
Tier only

Give your answer in standard form to 2 significant figures.

Density of sea water = 1.0×10^3 kg/m³

Gravitational field strength = 9.8 N/kg

Maths

The equation for the pressure due to a column of liquid is given on the Physics equations sheet. You need to be able to select and apply this equation.

Pressure = _____ Pa   [3 marks]

b Describe the direction of the force exerted by the seawater on the surface of the diver's body.

_____   [1 mark]

c The diver now dives to a greater depth below the surface of the sea. Describe how the pressure exerted on the diver by the sea water changes. Give a reason why the change occurs.

_____

_____

_____   [2 marks]

Atmospheric pressure

1. **a** Atmospheric pressure decreases with height above sea level (**Figure 14**).

   State which physical property of the air is changing to cause the trend in atmospheric pressure shown in **Figure 14**.

   _____ [1 mark]

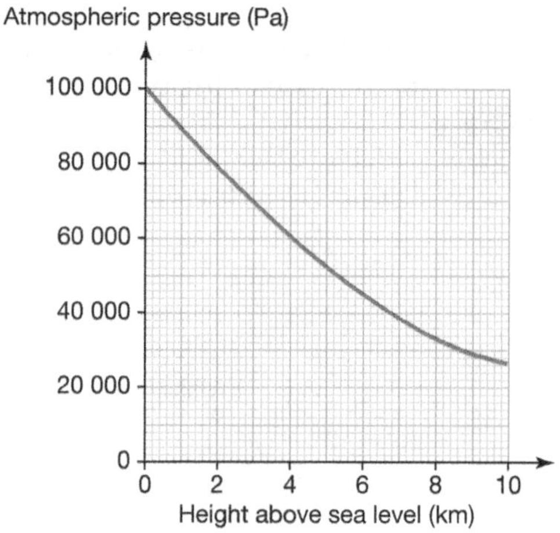

   Maths Skills

   b Mount Kilimanjaro, in Tanzania, is at a height of 6 km above sea level. Use **Figure 14** to determine the atmospheric pressure at the summit.

   Atmospheric pressure (Pa)

   Height above sea level (km)

   Figure 14

   Atmospheric pressure = _____ Pa   [1 mark]

   Maths Skills

   c The typical body surface area for an adult male is about $2\,m^2$. Calculate the total force exerted on an average adult male's body if he is at the summit of Mount Kilimanjaro.

   Force = _____ N   [3 marks]

2. Explain, in terms of the motion of gas molecules, why the force exerted by the atmosphere on the body of a person at altitude is less than at sea level.

   Literacy
   There are three marks here so make three points.

   _____

   _____

   _____

   _____ [3 marks]

Gravity and weight

1.

Maths Skills

The mass of a £1 coin is 8.8 g. Calculate its weight given that the gravitational field strength at the Earth's surface is 9.8 N/kg.

Give your answer to 2 significant figures.

Maths

You need to know the equation that relates the weight of an object to its mass and the gravitational field strength as you may not be given the equation in the question.

Weight = _____ N   [3 marks]

2.

Maths Skills

The weight of an object is measured using a newtonmeter and found to be 4.9 N.

Calculate the mass of the object. Give your answer in grams.

Mass = _____ g   [4 marks]

3. Explain how mass and weight are related.

_____

_____

_____

_____   [2 marks]

Resultant forces and Newton's first law

1.

Maths Skills

a **Figure 15** shows a small trolley subjected to three forces. Calculate the resultant force and state its direction.

15 N   8 N   3 N

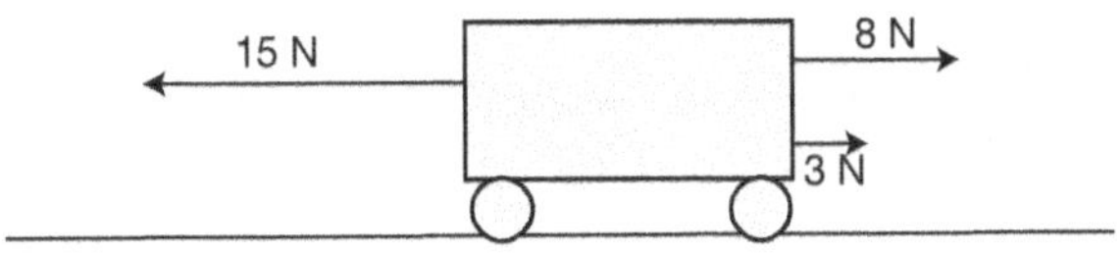

Figure 15

Resultant force = _____ N

Direction: _____   [2 marks]

b The 3 N force is now increased to 7 N. Calculate the resultant force acting on the trolley.

Resultant force = _____ N   [1 mark]

c The trolley was in motion when the 3 N force was increased to 7 N. Describe the motion of the trolley after the change in force has been made. Explain your answer.

_____

_____

_____   [3 marks]

2.

Higher
Tier only

Figure 16 shows a firework rocket travelling through the air. Draw a free body force diagram in the space next to **Figure 16** to show the three forces acting on the rocket.

Label each arrow with the name of the force.

[3 marks]

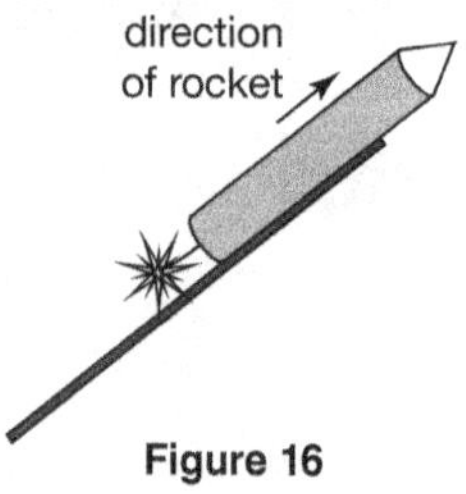

direction
of rocket

Figure 16

3.

A force, F, is shown in **Figure 17**, which is drawn to scale.

Maths
Skills

a Use **Figure 17** to determine the size of force F.

Force F = _____ N   [1 mark]

Higher
Tier only

b Draw arrows on **Figure 17** to show the horizontal and vertical components of force F. Label each arrow,   [2 marks]

Higher
Tier only

c Use **Figure 17** to determine the size of the horizontal and vertical components of force F.

Force F

Scale
5 N

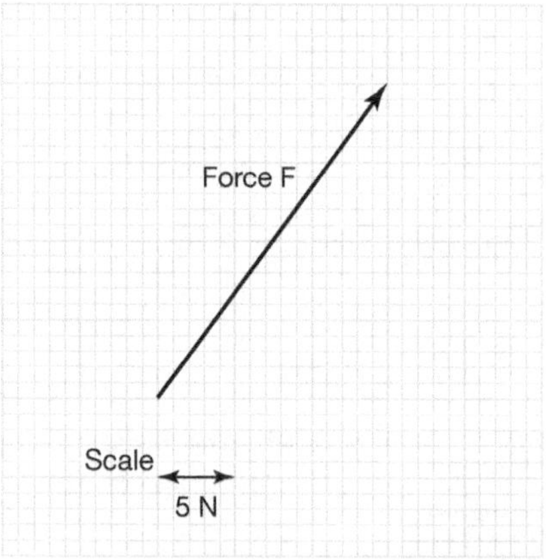

Figure 17

Horizontal component = _____ N

Vertical component = _____ N   [2 marks]

4. **a** An object is acted on by two 10 N forces. One force acts downwards and the other acts to the right.

Maths Skills

Higher Tier only

Draw a vector diagram on **Figure 18** to determine the size of the resultant force on the object.

Size of resultant force = _____ N [5 marks]

b Determine the direction of the resultant force. Label an angle on the diagram to show this direction. [1 mark]

Figure 18

Forces and acceleration

· ·

The engine driving force on a van is 3200 N. The friction and air resistance forces add up to 800 N. The mass of the van is 1000 kg. Calculate the van's acceleration. [4 marks]

Maths

You need to know the equation which links resultant force to mass and acceleration as you may not be given the equation in the question.

The resultant force on the van = 3200 − 800
                              = 2400 N [1 mark]

Resultant force $F = ma$

Substituting the data: $2400 = 1000 \times a$ [1 mark]

so acceleration a

$$= \frac{2400}{1000}$$ [1 mark]

$$= 2.4 \text{ m/s}^2$$ [1 mark]

1. The driving force on a truck generated by the engine is 4800 N. The total drag force acting on the truck is 1200 N. The mass of the truck is 3000 kg. Calculate the truck's acceleration.

acceleration = _____ m/s^2 [4 marks]

2. **a** The mass of a football is 420 g. Calculate the weight of the football in N.

Maths Skills

Give your answer to 2 significant figures.

Gravitational field strength = 9.8 N/kg.

Weight = _____ N [3 marks]

b The football is dropped from a height so that it falls vertically. As the football passes a point 1 m above the ground, the air resistance acting on the ball is 2.1 N.

Calculate the resultant force on the football at the instant it is 1 m above the ground.

Resultant force = _____ N   [2 marks]

c Calculate the acceleration of the football as it passes the 1 m height above the ground.

Give your answer to 2 significant figures.

Acceleration = _____ m/s²   [3 marks]

3.   **a** A cyclist is travelling along a straight road at a speed of 4.2 m/s. She then accelerates for 4.0 s until the bicycle reaches a speed of 6.2 m/s. Calculate the cyclist's acceleration.

Maths Skills

Acceleration = _____ m/s²   [2 marks]

b The combined mass of the cyclist and her bicycle is 60 kg. Calculate the resultant force acting on the cyclist during the 4.0 s of acceleration.

Resultant force = _____ N   [2 marks]

c The average total drag forces on the cyclist during the acceleration are 20 N. Calculate the driving force generated by the cyclist.

Driving force = _____ N   [2 marks]

4.   A student uses an air track, with glider and light gates, to investigate the relationship between the resultant force acting on the glider and its acceleration (**Figure 19**).

Required practical

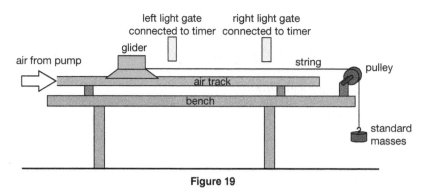

Figure 19

When the glider is released at the left end of the track, it is accelerated and passes through both light gates.

a Describe how the resultant force acting on the glider is determined.

_____

_____ [1 mark]

b The student releases the glider and records the measurements in **Table 1**.

Length of upper section of the glider / m	Reading on timer connected to left light gate / s	Reading on timer connected to the right gate / s
0.10	0.50	0.25

Table 1

Use the information in the table to determine the speed of the glider through the left light gate and the right light gate.

Speed through left gate = _____ m/s

Speed through right gate = _____ m/s   [5 marks]

c The distance between the light gates is 0.50 m. Calculate the acceleration of the glider. Select the correct equation from the Physics equations sheet.

acceleration = _____ m/s²   [3 marks]

d The student changes the resultant force acting on the glider and calculates the new acceleration of the glider. The student repeats this process to produce ten data sets of acceleration and resultant force.

Identify the independent and dependent variables.

Independent variable: _____

Dependent variable: _____   [2 marks]

e   The student predicts that the acceleration of the glider should be directly proportional to the resultant force

What features of a graph of acceleration versus resultant force would show that the student's prediction is correct?

_____

_____ [2 marks]

Terminal velocity

1. **Figure 20** shows three free-body diagrams showing the forces acting on an object.

Which is the correct free-body diagram for an objecting falling at its terminal velocity?

Tick **one** box.

A ☐   B ☐   C ☐   [1 mark]

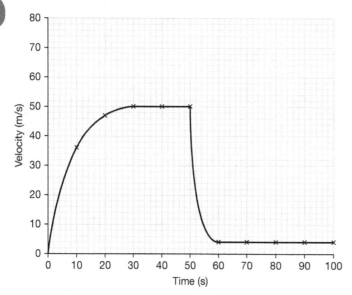

Figure 20

2. **Figure 21** shows the change in velocity of a sky diver before and after his parachute is opened.

Maths Skills

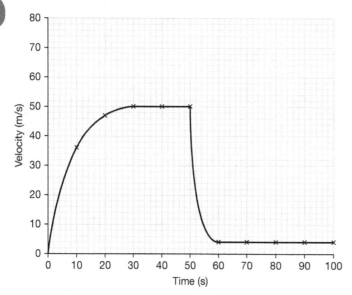

Figure 21

a When the sky diver opens his parachute he decelerates rapidly. Use **Figure 21** to determine the sky diver's terminal velocity values before and after he opens his parachute.

Terminal velocity before opening parachute = _____ m/s

Terminal velocity after opening parachute = _____ m/s   [2 marks]

b Use **Figure 21** to estimate the sky diver's acceleration 20 s after the start of the jump.

Show clearly on the graph how you determine your answer.

Maths

The gradient of a velocity–time graph gives acceleration.

Acceleration = _____ m/s²   [2 marks]

c Use **Figure 21** to describe the changes in the sky diver's acceleration during the first 40 s of the jump.

Explain what causes the changes in acceleration and why the sky diver reaches a terminal velocity.

_____

_____

_____

_____

_____

_____

_____   [6 marks]

Newton's third law

1. **a** State Newton's third law.

_____

_____   [1 mark]

b Figure **22** shows the two forces, **X** and **Y**, acting on a book resting on a table.

What type of force is **X**? State what object is exerting this force.

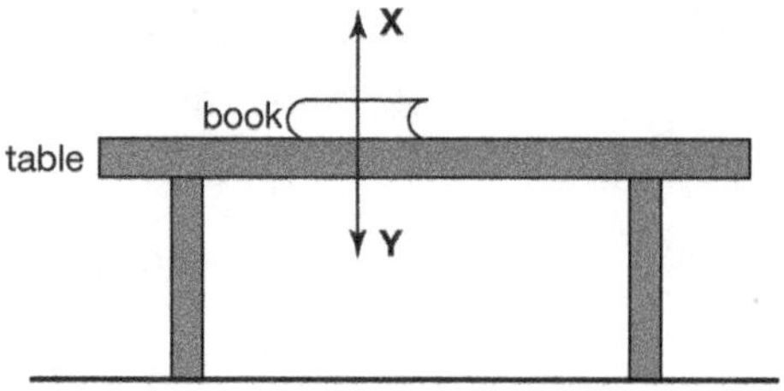

_____

_____ [2 marks]

Figure 22

c What type of force is **Y**? State what object is exerting this force.

_____

_____ [2 marks]

d Describe the force that forms a Newton's third law pair with force **X**.

Name the object exerting the force and the object that the force is acting on.

_____

_____

_____ [3 marks]

e Describe the force that forms a Newton's third law pair with force **Y**. Name the object exerting the force and the object that the force is acting on.

_____

_____

_____ [3 marks]

Work done and energy transfer

. . . .

Worked Example ▶ A load is dragged 10 m from the bottom to the top of a ramp by a cable attached to a winch (**Figure 23**). The tension in the cable is 800 N. The time taken to move the load 10 m along the ramp is 20 s.

Calculate the work done by the winch and its useful output power. [4 marks]

Maths

You need to know the equation that relates work done to force and distance moved in the direction of the force as you may not be given the equation in the question.

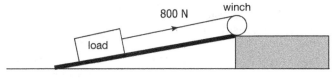

Figure 23

Work done = $Fs = 800 \times 10$ [1 mark]

= 8000 J   [1 mark]

Useful output power = $\dfrac{\text{work done}}{\text{time}} = \dfrac{8000}{20}$ [1 mark]

= 400 W   [1 mark]

1.   **a**   A load is dragged 20 m from the bottom to the top of a ramp by a cable attached to a winch (**Figure 24**). The tension in the cable is 0.60 kN. The time taken to move the load 20 m along the ramp is 20 s.

Maths Skills

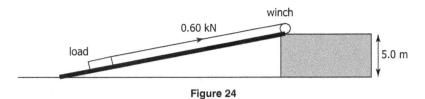

Figure 24

Calculate the work done by the winch and its useful output power.

Work done = _____ J

Power = _____ W   [5 marks]

b   The load has a mass of 200 kg. Calculate the increase in the load's store of gravitational potential energy when it has reached the top of the ramp.

Gravitational field strength = 9.8 N/kg

Increase in gravitational potential energy = _____ J   [2 marks]

c   Suggest why the increase in gravitational potential energy is less than the work done by the winch.

_____   [1 mark]

2.

a A lift in a building has a mass of 600 kg. There are 5 passengers of average mass 80 kg inside the lift.

Calculate the force needed to raise the lift at a steady speed.

Gravitational field strength = 9.8 N/kg

> **Remember**
> According to Newton's First law, the force needed to lift a mass at a steady speed is equal to the weight of the mass.

Force = _____ N   [2 marks]

b The lift takes the passengers from the ground floor to the top floor of the building in 10 s. The distance travelled is 10 m.

Calculate the useful output power of the winch raising the lift.

> **Maths**
> Some multi-step calculation questions require you to use two equations.

Power = _____ W   [4 marks]

3.

a An aircraft flies at a constant speed. The thrust from its engine is 5.0 kN.

Calculate the work done by the aircraft's engine as it travels 1000 m.

Work = _____ J   [2 marks]

b The speed of the aircraft is 100 m/s. Calculate the time taken for the aircraft to fly 1000 m.

Time = _____ s   [1 mark]

c Calculate the useful output power of the aircraft engine.

Power = _____ W   [2 marks]

Stopping distance

1. The stopping distance of a car can be calculated from:

Stopping distance = thinking distance + braking distance

a State what is meant by **thinking distance**. Give one factor that can affect thinking distance.

_____

_____ [2 marks]

b State what is meant by **braking distance**. Give one factor that can affect braking distance.

_____

_____ [2 marks]

Maths Skills

c The graph in **Figure 25** shows how thinking distance and braking distance for a typical car vary with speed.

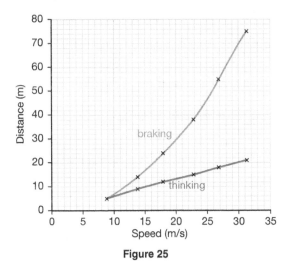

Figure 25

Use **Figure 25** to determine the stopping distance for a car travelling at 15 m/s.

Stopping distance = _____ m [1 mark]

d Use **Figure 25** to determine the stopping distance for a car travelling at 30 m/s.

Stopping distance = _____ m [1 mark]

e A student makes the following prediction:

Doubling a car's speed causes the stopping distance to double

Compare your answers to parts (c) and (d) to determine if the student's prediction is correct.

Give a reason for your answer.

_____

_____

_____ [2 marks]

Worked Example

A car of mass 800 kg is travelling at a speed of 10 m/s. A hazard appears and the driver applies his brakes. The car's braking distance is 8.0 m.

Remember

The work done by the brakes to stop a car is equal to the car's original store of kinetic energy.

a Calculate the car's initial kinetic energy. [2 marks]

b Estimate the braking force created by the car's brakes. [2 marks]

a Kinetic energy = $\frac{1}{2} mv^2 = \frac{1}{2} \times 800 \times 10^2$ [1 mark]

$= 40\,000$ J [1 mark]

b Work done to stop the car is equal to the car's original store of kinetic energy.

Work done = 40000 = braking force × distance

400000 = braking force × 8.0

braking force = $\frac{40\,000}{8.0}$ [1 mark]

$= 5000$ N [1 mark]

2. A van is being driven at a constant speed of 20 m/s. A hazard appears and the driver applies the brakes. The thinking distance is 14 m.

a Calculate the value of the driver's reaction time.

Reaction time = _____ s [2 marks]

b The mass of the van and driver is 1000 kg. The van's braking distance is 40 m.

Calculate the average braking force generated by the van's brakes.

Braking force = _____ N   [5 marks]

c Friction between the brakes and the wheels, and friction between the tyres and the road bring the car to a stop. Describe the energy changes that occur. Include in your answer the effect on the brakes when a car brakes suddenly.

_____

_____

_____   [3 marks]

Force and extension

A force of 2.0 N stretches a spring by 4.0 cm. Calculate the spring constant of the spring in N/m.   [4 marks]

Maths

You need to know the equation that links the force applied to a spring, to its spring constant and extension, as you may not be given this equation in the question.

Change 4.0 cm to 0.040 m   [1 mark]

Use force $F = ke$

2.0 = k × 0.040   [1 mark]

Rearranging gives

$k = \frac{2.0}{0.040}$ [1 mark]

= 50 N/m   [1 mark]

1. **Figure 26** shows a spring before and after it has been stretched. Note that the spring has not been stretched beyond its limit of proportionality.

Maths
Skills

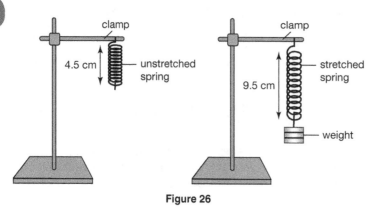

Figure 26

a Describe the two forces that act on the spring to cause it to be extended.

_____

_____

_____ [2 marks]

b The weight attached to the spring in **Figure 26** is 2.0 N. Calculate the spring constant of the spring in N/m.

Spring constant = _____ N/m [4 marks]

c Calculate the elastic potential energy stored in the spring. Use the correct equation from the Physics equations

Maths

The equation for elastic potential energy is given on the Physics equations sheet. You need to be able to select and apply this equation.

Elastic potential energy = _____ J [2 marks]

2.

A student is provided with the apparatus shown in **Figure 27** to investigate the relationship between force and extension for a spring. The student is only given weights up to 3.0 N to prevent the spring being stretched beyond its limit of proportionality.

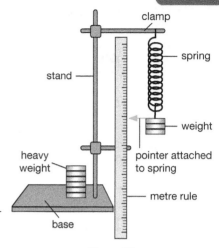

Figure 27

a Describe how the student should use the apparatus to generate force and extension data for the spring. You should include what steps you could take to minimise possible sources of error.

_____

_____

_____

_____

_____

_____

_____ [4 marks]

b **Table 2** shows the student's force and extension data.

Force/N	Extension/cm
0	0
0.5	1.5
1.0	3.0
1.5	4.5
2.0	6.0
2.5	7.4
3.0	9.0

Table 2

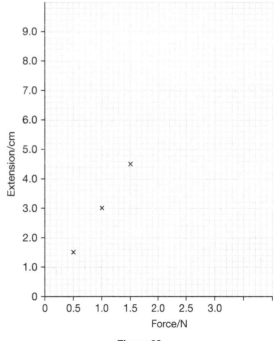

Figure 28

The first three points have already been plotted on the graph of extension versus force shown in **Figure 28**.

Plot the remaining three points on the graph in **Figure 28**. [3 marks]

c Draw a best fit line on the graph in **Figure 28**. [1 mark]

d What can be concluded from the graph about the relation between extension and force for this spring?

Give a reason for your answer.

_____

_____

_____ [2 marks]

e Determine the gradient of the best fit line you have drawn on **Figure 28**.

Give your answer to 2 significant figures.

Gradient = _____ cm/N [2 marks]

f The spring constant, in N/cm, can be found from:

$$spring\ constant = \frac{1}{gradient}$$

Determine the spring constant of the spring in N/cm.

Give your answer to 2 significant figures.

Spring constant = _____ N/cm [2 marks]

Momentum

1.

Higher Tier only

a State whether momentum is a vector or scalar quantity.

_____ [1 mark]

Maths Skills

b A car of mass 850 kg is travelling at 36 km/h on a straight section of road. Calculate its momentum in kg m/s.

Momentum = _____ kg m/s [3 marks]

Maths

You need to learn the equation for momentum as it may not be given to you in the question.

2.

Higher Tier only

Maths Skills

The velocity time graph for a car of mass 800 kg is shown in **Figure 29**. Determine the car's momentum change between time = 10 s and time = 20 s.

Momentum = _____ kg m/s

[2 marks]

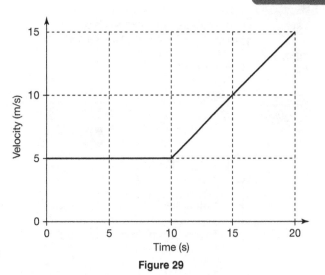

Figure 29

3.

Higher Tier only

Maths Skills

A subatomic particle is moving in a straight line with momentum = 2.4×10^{-21} kg m/s. The mass of the particle is 1.7×10^{-27} kg. Calculate the velocity of the particle.

Give your answer in standard form to 2 significant figures.

Velocity = _____ m/s   [4 marks]

Conservation of momentum

Higher Tier only

Figure 30 shows two trolleys a moment before they collide.

mass = 0.50 kg   mass = 0.20 kg
velocity = 1.0 m/s   velocity = 0.50 m/s

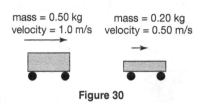

Figure 30

a Calculate the total momentum before the collision.
[2 marks]

b Calculate the velocity, v, of the larger trolley immediately after the collision if the small trolley moves off with a velocity of 0.80 m/s.   [4 marks]

a Total momentum = $(0.50 \times 1.0) + (0.20 \times 0.50)$ [1 mark]

= 0.60 kg m/s   [1 mark]

b Total momentum after the collision = total momentum before collision   [1 mark]

$(0.50 \times v) + (0.20 \times 0.80) = 0.60$ [1 mark]

Gives velocity $v = \frac{0.60 - 0.16}{0.5}$ [1 mark]

= 0.88 m/s   [1 mark]

1.

Higher
Tier only

Maths
Skills

On a snooker table, the white ball collides head on with a
stationary black ball (**Figure 31**).

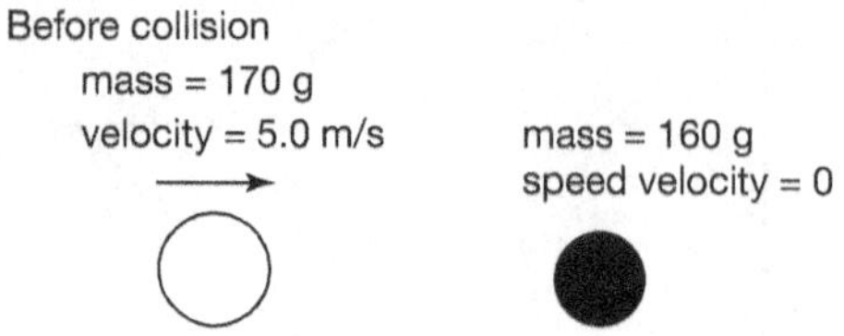

Remember

The total momentum after
a collision is equal to the
total momentum before the
collision.

Before collision
    mass = 170 g
    velocity = 5.0 m/s   mass = 160 g
                              speed velocity = 0

Figure 31

a Calculate the momentum of the white ball before the collision.

Give your answer in kg m/s.

Momentum = _____ kg m/s   [2 marks]

b After the collision, the black ball has a velocity of 4.0 m/s. Calculate the velocity of the
white ball after the collision. Give your answer to 2 significant figures.

Velocity = _____ m/s   [5 marks]

2.

Higher
Tier only

Maths
Skills

Figure 32 shows a van and a car a moment before the van collides with the car.

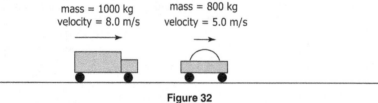

    mass = 1000 kg   mass = 800 kg
    velocity = 8.0 m/s   velocity = 5.0 m/s

Figure 32

a Calculate the total momentum before the collision.

Momentum = _____ kg m/s   [2 marks]

b On impact the bumpers on the van and the car lock together. Calculate their combined
velocity immediately after the impact.

Combined velocity = _____ m/s   [5 marks]

Rate of change of momentum

 In a laboratory test, the impact forces on the head of a crash dummy are measured with and without a cycle helmet. In both cases the momentum change of the crash dummy's head is 10 kg m/s. The time of the collision without a cycle helmet is 0.015 s and with a cycle helmet is 0.025 s.

Higher Tier only

Maths

The equation which links force, change in momentum and time is on the Physics equations sheet. You need to be able to select and apply this equation.

Calculate the impact force for the collisions without and with a cycle helmet. [4 marks]

Without a cycle helmet:

$$\text{force} = \frac{\text{change in momentum}}{\text{time}} = \frac{10}{0.015}$$ [1 mark]

$$= 667 \text{ N}$$ [1 mark]

With a cycle helmet:

$$\text{force} = \frac{\text{change in momentum}}{\text{time}} = \frac{10}{0.025}$$ [1 mark]

$$= 400 \text{ N}$$ [1 mark]

1.

Higher Tier only

a A gymnast of mass 50 kg jumps down from a vaulting box on to a crash mat. The velocity of the gymnast as he hits the mat is 5.0 m/s.

Calculate the momentum of the gymnast as he strikes the mat.

Momentum = _____ kg m/s   [2 marks]

b The mat brings the gymnast to a stop in 0.50 s. Calculate the impact force on the gymnast. Use the correct equation from the Physics equations sheet.

Force = _____ N   [2 marks]

c If the gymnast had landed on the wooden floor of the gym, without the crash mat, he would have come to a stop much more suddenly. Explain how this would have affected the impact force on the gymnast.

_____

_____

_____ [3 marks]

2.

Higher Tier only

Maths Skills

At a crash test centre, two cars, A and B, are used in test crashes with a crash barrier. Each car comes to a stop on impact with the crash barrier. The data from the two crashes is shown in **Table 4**.

Car	Mass in kg	Impact velocity in m/s	Impact time/s
A	1000	6.0	0.10
B	800	8.0	0.10

Table 4

a Calculate the rate of change of momentum for each car.

Car A's rate of change of momentum = _____ kg m/s²

Car B's rate of change of momentum = _____ kg m/s²   [4 marks]

b State which car experiences the greatest impact force. Explain your answer.

_____

_____   [2 marks]

Transverse and longitudinal waves

1. How do the particles move in a longitudinal wave? Tick **one** box.

From side to side ☐

In the same direction as the wave movement ☐

At right angles to the direction of the wave movement ☐ [1 mark]

2. Which of these travels as a transverse wave? Tick **two** boxes.

Microwaves ☐

Seismic P waves ☐

Seismic S waves ☐

Ultrasound ☐ [1 mark]

3. Sound travels through air as a longitudinal wave. Describe the differences between a region of compression and a region of rarefaction in a sound wave passing through air.

_____

_____

_____ [2 marks]

4. A vibrating guitar string produces sound waves that travel through the air from the string to listeners.

What evidence can you give that air is not carried away from the string as the sound waves travel?

_____

_____ [1 mark]

Frequency and period

Worked Example Calculate the period of a sound wave of frequency 4 Hz. Use the correct equation from the Physics equations sheet. [1 mark]

Time period $T = \frac{1}{f}$

$$= \frac{1}{4} \text{ or } 0.25 \text{ s} \qquad \text{[1 mark]}$$

Maths

The equation relating period (T) to frequency (f), $T = \frac{1}{f}$, is given on the Physics equations sheet. You are expected to be able to select and apply this equation.

1. In music, the note 'middle A' has a frequency of 440 Hz.

Maths Skills Find the period of sound waves of this frequency. Use the correct equation from the Physics equations sheet.

Give your answer in milliseconds to 2 significant figures.

Period = _____ ms [4 marks]

2. A seismic wave produces ground shaking with a period of 0.4 s. What is the frequency of this seismic wave?

Maths Skills

Frequency = _____ Hz [3 marks]

3. Damage to a car's wheels causes the steering wheel to vibrate at 15 Hz. What is the time period of these vibrations?

Maths Skills Give your answer to 2 significant figures.

Period = _____ s [3 marks]

4. The range of normal human hearing is from 20 Hz to 20 kHz. Calculate the **maximum** period of an audible wave.

Maths Skills

Period = _____ s [2 marks]

Wave calculations

An ultrasound wave in air has a frequency of 170 kHz. What is its wavelength?

Maths

The speed of sound in air is 340 m/s.   [4 marks]

170 kHz = 170 000 Hz   [1 mark]

$v = f\lambda$ so $340 = 170\,000 \times \lambda$ [1 mark]

$\lambda = \frac{340}{170\,000}$ [1 mark]

$= 0.0020$ m   [1 mark]

The equation that links wave speed to frequency and wavelength is $v = f\lambda$. You need to learn this equation as it may not be given to you in the question.

1. BBC Radio 5 Live broadcasts at a frequency of 909 kHz.

Maths Skills

Calculate the wavelength of these radio waves.

The speed of light in air is 3.0×10^8 m/s.

Wavelength = _____ m   [4 marks]

2. A student produces water waves in a ripple tank using a motor attached to a straight dipper. The student takes a photo of the waves with a ruler held just above the waves.

Required practical

a Describe how the student could use this photo to make an accurate estimate of the wavelength of the water waves.

_____

_____   [1 mark]

b Describe how the student could estimate the speed of a single wave.

_____

_____   [2 marks]

Without changing the frequency of the motor, the student made measurements of the speed of several waves. See **Table 1**.

Table 1

Experiment number	Speed (m/s)
1	0.232
2	0.250
3	0.241

c Suggest **one** reason for the variation in the measured wave speeds.

_____ [1 mark]

d Calculate the mean of the wave speeds.

Mean speed = _____ m/s [1 mark]

e Calculate the uncertainty in the measurements.

Uncertainty = _____ m/s [2 marks]

Maths

The range of values about the mean gives an estimate of the uncertainty in the measurement. We write the uncertainty as a plus or minus.

3. Sound can be transmitted from one material to another. Sound waves travel faster in a metal than in air. Explain how a change in speed affects the wavelength of the sound wave.

_____

_____ [2 marks]

Worked Example

A mosquito flaps its front wings 300 times in 0.5 seconds. Calculate the wavelength of the sound emitted by the mosquito's wings.

The speed of sound in air is 330 m/s. [4 marks]

Frequency of the sound wave produced
$= \frac{300}{0.5}$ s = 600 Hz [1 mark]

using $v = f\lambda$, 330 = 600 × λ [1 mark]

$\lambda = \frac{330}{600}$ [1 mark]

= 0.55 m [1 mark]

Problem solving

In some calculation questions, you may have to use more than one equation. Write down your working for each part of the problem. By showing correct working you will get some marks even if your final answer is wrong.

4. Visible light has a range of wavelengths from around 400 nm to 700 nm. All electromagnetic waves travel through space at 300 000 000 m/s.

Maths Skills

Determine the minimum period of visible light.

Synoptic

Give your answer to 1 significant figure.

Period = _____ s   [6 marks]

Reflection and refraction of waves

1. A ray of light in air strikes a mirror. Which of the following occurs at the surface of the mirror? Tick **one** box.

Absorption ☐

Reflection ☐

Transmission ☐   [1 mark]

2. Describe what happens when a ray of light in air strikes an opaque object.

_____

_____   [2 marks]

3. Describe what happens to rays of light reflected from a rough surface.

_____

_____   [2 marks]

4.

Required
practical

A student is asked to investigate how the direction of a ray of light changes as it enters and leaves blocks of different materials (**Figure 2**). They use a protractor to measure the angle of incidence where the ray enters the block.

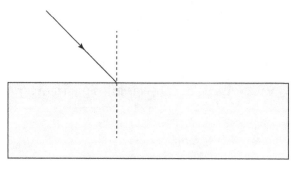

Figure 2

a Label the angle of incidence on **Figure 2**.

The light ray travels through and exits the block.   [1 mark]

b Describe how the student should find the angle at which the ray of light is transmitted through the block.

_____

_____

_____

_____

_____   [3 marks]

The student obtains some values for angles of incidence and angles of refraction for blocks made of two different materials. See **Table 2**.

Block 1		Block 2	
Angle of incidence (°)	Angle of refraction (°)	Angle of incidence (°)	Angle of refraction (°)
30	19	30	20
35	22	35	23
40	25	40	26
60	34	60	36

Table 2

c The student concludes that for the same angle of incidence the angles of refraction are slightly different for the two materials.

Suggest **one** reason why this may not be a valid conclusion. Explain your answer.

_____

_____   [2 marks]

d Suggest what extra data is needed for the student to be more certain that the conclusion is correct.

_____

_____ [2 marks]

5. Light is refracted as it passes from air into water. Give the reason why this occurs.

Higher Tier only _____ [1 mark]

Sound waves

. . . .

1. State the range of normal human hearing. [1 mark]

Higher Tier only Range = _____ Hz to _____ Hz

2. State what happens to the ear drum when sound waves travelling in air enter the ear.

Higher Tier only _____ [1 mark]

3. Explain what happens to the air surrounding a drum skin when the drum skin vibrates.

Higher Tier only _____

_____ [2 marks]

4. A teacher asks a class to design a method to measure the speed of sound waves in air. One student suggests using a stopwatch to measure the time taken to hear an echo from a sharp clap made in front of a large cliff.

a Suggest why this method is unlikely to produce an accurate result.

_____

_____ [1 mark]

b Suggest **one** improvement to this method.

Explain why this would improve the accuracy of the measurement.

_____

_____

_____ [3 marks]

5. Certain parts of the inner ear can only vibrate at a limited range of frequencies. Explain why this limits the frequency range humans can hear.

Higher Tier only

_____

_____ [2 marks]

Ultrasound and echo sounding

1. Give **one** difference between ultrasound and the sounds that humans can hear.

Higher Tier only

_____ [1 mark]

2. Describe three things that happen when ultrasound waves travelling in a solid strike a boundary with another material.

Higher Tier only

_____

_____

_____ [3 marks]

Literacy
There are three marks here so make three points. You have to say more than just 'reflected'.

> **Worked Example** A ship sends out a pulse of ultrasound and detects an echo from the seabed 0.4 s later. The speed of sound in sea water is 1500 m/s.
>
> Calculate the depth of the water below the ship. [3 marks]
>
> Use the equation: distance travelled = speed × time
>
> distance travelled = 1500 × 0.4 [1 mark]
>
> = 600 m [1 mark]
>
> Halve the distance (because the pulse travels to the seabed and back):

98 depth = 600 m / 2 = 300 m [1 mark]

3. A ship sends out a pulse of ultrasound and detects an echo from a shoal of fish 240 ms later.

Higher Tier only

a The speed of sound in sea water is 1500 m/s. How far has the ultrasound pulse travelled?

Maths Skills

Distance travelled = _____ m   [3 marks]

b How deep is the shoal of fish?

Depth = _____ m   [1 mark]

4. Ultrasound waves are used to detect internal cracks in a piece of metal. The ultrasound transmitter and detector are fixed to the surface of the metal. When ultrasound waves reach the crack, some are reflected back to the detector.

Higher Tier only

Figure 3 shows the screen of an oscilloscope used to detect the transmitted pulse and the reflection, A. Each horizontal division represents 20 microseconds.

Maths Skills

Transmitted pulse

A

The speed of sound in the metal is 6000 m/s. Calculate how far the crack is from the surface.

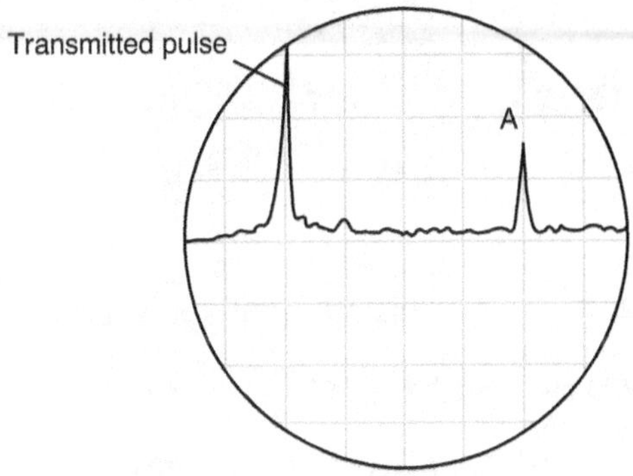

Figure 3

Distance to crack = _____ m   [5 marks]

5. Explain how an ultrasound scan can produce an image showing different tissues, such as bone and muscle, at different depths inside the body.

Higher Tier only

_____

_____

_____

_____

_____   [4 marks]

6. Compare ultrasound and ultraviolet waves.

Higher Tier only

Synoptic

_____

_____

_____

_____

_____

_____   [4 marks]

Seismic waves

1. Which statement below about seismic waves is correct? Tick **one** box.

Higher
Tier only

Both P and S-waves can travel through solids and liquids ☐

S-waves can travel through solids but not through liquids ☐

P-waves can travel through solids but not through liquids ☐

Neither P nor S-waves can travel through liquids ☐   [1 mark]

2. P-waves and S-waves travel at different speeds in the same material. Give **two** other differences between P and S-waves.

Higher
Tier only

_____

_____   [2 marks]

3. Seismic waves from an earthquake can be detected on the Earth's surface after they have travelled into the Earth and back towards the surface.

Higher
Tier only

Synoptic

a Explain why seismic waves can change direction suddenly as they pass through different parts of the Earth.

_____

_____   [2 marks]

b   Earthquakes produce both P- and S-waves. There are regions on the Earth's surface where P-waves but not S-waves are detected from an earthquake.

What does this provide evidence for? Tick **one** box.

Part of the Earth's core is liquid ☐

Part of the Earth's core is solid ☐

There is a sudden change in P-wave velocity at the Earth's core ☐

There is a sudden change in S-wave velocity at the Earth's core ☐   [1 mark]

The electromagnetic spectrum

1.   Give **two** differences between microwaves and radio waves.

1 _____

2 _____   [2 marks]

2.   Give **two** differences between infrared and ultraviolet waves.

1 _____

2 _____   [2 marks]

3.   All electromagnetic waves transfer energy from the source of the waves. Where is this energy transferred to?

_____   [1 mark]

4.   The waves in the electromagnetic spectrum have a continuous range of wavelengths.

Which of these waves has the shortest wavelength? Tick **one** box.

Red light, 400 nm ☐

Far infrared light, 9 μm ☐

Radar, 9 mm ☐   [1 mark]

5. Compare the properties and uses of gamma rays and X-rays.

Synoptic

_____

_____

_____

_____

_____

_____

_____

_____ [4 marks]

Refraction and wavefronts

1. Radio waves pass directly through the lower atmosphere but can be refracted when they enter the upper atmosphere.

Higher Tier only State why the direction of the wave changes.

_____ [1 mark]

2. A ray of light in air enters a rectangular glass block at an angle and is refracted. **Figure 4** shows wave fronts approaching the block.

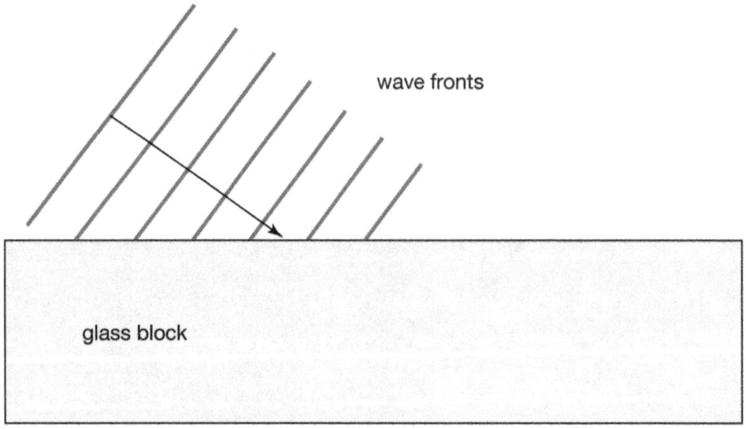

wave fronts

glass block

Figure 4

a Which statement about the refracted wave fronts is true? Tick **one** box.

Continue in the original direction, parallel to each other ☐

Continue in the original direction but spread out away from each other ☐

Change direction, but stay parallel to each other ☐

Change direction and also spread out away from each other ☐ [1 mark]

b Draw at least **two** refracted wave fronts inside the block in **Figure 4** to show the refraction of the wave. [2 marks]

Higher Tier only **c** When the wave fronts enter the glass block they slow down.

Explain why this causes the wave fronts to change direction.

_____

_____

_____

_____ [2 marks]

Emission and absorption of infrared radiation

1. Which statement is true? Tick **one** box.

Only very hot objects emit and absorb infrared radiation ☐

All hot objects emit infrared radiation but only cool objects absorb infrared radiation ☐

All objects both emit and absorb infrared radiation, whether they are hot or cool ☐ [1 mark]

2. A student has four aluminium cans with the following outer surfaces:

Required practical

polished aluminium   dull aluminium   shiny black paint   dull/matt black paint

The student filled each can with cold water at 5 °C, placed a lid on each can and placed the cans in direct sunlight. See **Figure 5**.

She measured the time taken for the temperature of the water in each can to increase to 15 °C.

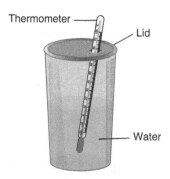

Figure 5

a Identify the dependent and independent variables in this experiment.

Dependent: _____

Independent: _____ [2 marks]

b The student used the same starting temperature for each can. Suggest **two** other variables that should be controlled for this experiment.

1 _____

2 _____ [2 marks]

3.

Higher Tier only

When solar radiation strikes a glass window, it is partly reflected, partly absorbed by the glass and partly transmitted. **Figure 6** shows how the percentage of the radiation that is transmitted by the glass depends on its wavelength.

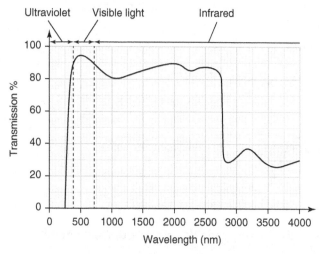

Figure 6

a Determine the range of wavelengths that are transmitted through glass with the **least** absorption or reflection.

Range = _____ nm to _____ nm

[1 mark]

Command words

When the question says **determine** you must use the data you are given to obtain an answer.

b Determine **two** ranges of wavelengths which are strongly absorbed by glass.

1 _____ nm to _____ nm

2 _____ nm to _____ nm   [2 marks]

c Optical fibres made of glass are used to transmit infrared signals used in data communications. An engineer says that not all infrared wavelengths can be used to transmit the signals. Use data from the graph to explain why the engineer is correct.

_____

_____

_____   [2 marks]

Synoptic **d** Use the graph to explain why glass appears colourless.

_____

_____   [2 marks]

4.

Required practical

A student uses the apparatus in **Figure 7** to investigate how the emission of infrared radiation from the different sides of a metal container depends on the colour and nature of the surface.

The container is filled with boiling water. The sides of the container have equal areas.

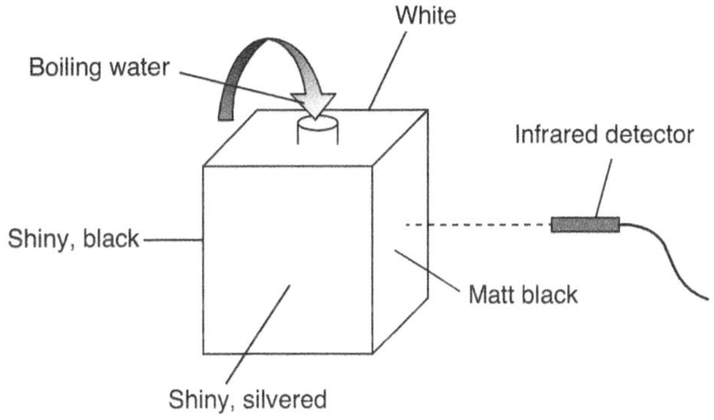

Figure 7

a Suggest **one** other variable that should be controlled for this experiment.

_____   [1 mark]

b After pouring in the hot water, the student waits one minute before pointing the infrared detector at each of the four sides. State why they wait.

_____   [1 mark]

c The sensor measures the intensity of infrared radiation emitted from each surface, in watts per square metre (W/m²). Why should the student use a bar chart, not a line graph, to present their results?

_____   [1 mark]

Uses and hazards of the electromagnetic spectrum

1. Some combination microwave ovens contain an electric grill. Name the **two** types of electromagnetic waves that these ovens use to cook food.

   1 _____

   2 _____   [2 marks]

2. Ultraviolet lamps are used in sun beds to give a tan. State **one** hazard of using a sun bed.

   _____   [1 mark]

3. High-frequency microwaves have frequencies which are absorbed by water molecules, reflected from metals but can pass through glass and most plastics.

   Higher Tier only

   a Suggest why microwaves are suitable for cooking food. Use ideas about energy transfer in your answer.

   _____

   _____   [2 marks]

   b Give **one** reason why food cooked in a microwave oven is placed in a glass or plastic container.

   _____   [1 mark]

4. Sunglasses are often advertised as having ultraviolet protection. Describe how the different wavelengths of electromagnetic radiation in sunlight are affected by these sunglasses.

   Higher Tier only

   _____

   _____   [2 marks]

5. Some cameras used by police officers can produce images of people in the dark.

   a Name the type of electromagnetic waves that these cameras detect.

   _____   [1 mark]

b State why these cameras can detect people in darkness, when there is no source of light to reflect any objects.

_____ [1 mark]

Synoptic

c Glass absorbs the type of electromagnetic waves used by these cameras. For this reason, the cover over the sensor is made of plexiglass, a type of plastic. The plexiglass can be coloured black and the sensor will still work.

Explain how this is possible.

_____

_____

_____ [2 marks]

Radio waves

1. State how radio waves are produced.

_____ [1 mark]

2. When radio waves are absorbed by a conductor, this produces an electrical current. Describe how this current is used by a radio receiver circuit to 'pick up' radio waves of a certain frequency.

_____ [1 mark]

3. Radio waves are not absorbed by the atmosphere. Explain why radio waves are suitable for transmitting television programs. Use ideas about energy transfer in your answer.

_____

_____ [2 marks]

Colour

1. The waves in the visible light spectrum have a continuous range of wavelengths. The shortest wavelength that the eyes can detect is 390 nm.

   a What is this wavelength in m, in standard form? Tick **one** box.

   3.9×10^{-7} m ☐ 3.9×10^{-11} m ☐

   3.9×10^{-9} m ☐ 390×10^{-9} m ☐   [1 mark]

   b This light has a frequency of 770 THz.

   What is this frequency in Hz, in standard form? Tick **one** box.

   Remember

   'tera' is a prefix that is equal to 1×10^{12}. So $1 \text{THz} = 10^{12}$ Hz.

   7.7×10^{14} Hz ☐ 7.7×10^{12} Hz ☐

   7.7×10^{10} Hz ☐ 770×10^{12} Hz ☐   [1 mark]

2. Explain how a green filter turns white light into green light.

   _____

   _____ [2 marks]

3. Sunlight contains a spectrum of different colours. A flower appears red in sunlight.

   a Explain what happens to the sunlight that is incident on the flower.

   _____

   _____ [2 marks]

   b State what colour the flower would appear if blue light was shone on it. Give a reason for your answer.

   _____

   _____

   [2 marks]

   Common misconception

   A common mistake is to think that red objects appear red because they absorb red light. However, if they absorbed red light, then red light wouldn't be able to continue into your eyes.

Lenses

1. Draw the symbol for a convex lens. [1 mark]

2. Describe what a convex lens does to parallel rays of light.

_____

_____ [2 marks]

3. Describe an experiment you could carry out to measure the focal length of a convex lens. You may draw a diagram to illustrate your answer.

_____

_____

_____

_____

_____

_____ [4 marks]

4. **Figure 8** shows an object 2 cm tall, at a distance of 2 cm from a converging lens. The lens has a focal length of 6 cm.

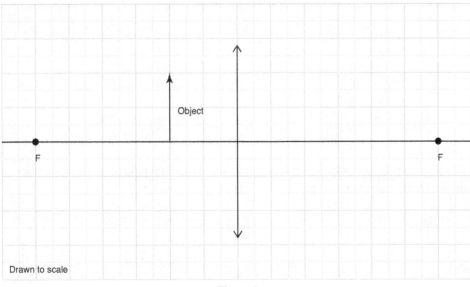

Drawn to scale

Figure 8

a Use a ruler to draw rays that can be used to locate the position of the image. Use an arrow to represent the image. [4 marks]

Maths

The equation magnification
$= \dfrac{\text{image height}}{\text{object height}}$ is on the
Physics equations sheet.
You should be able to select
and apply the equation.

Maths Skills

b Calculate the magnification of the lens.

Use the correct equation from the Physics equations sheet.

Magnification = _____ [2 marks]

c State whether the image is real or virtual.

_____ [1 mark]

5. **Figure 9** shows an object 3 cm tall, at a distance of 6 cm from a converging lens. The lens has a focal length of 2 cm.

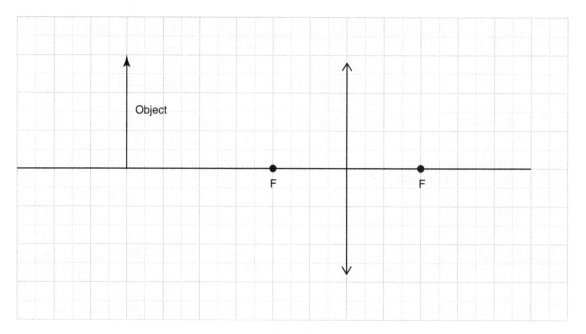

Object

F

F

Figure 9

a Use a ruler to draw rays that can be used to locate the position of the image. Use an arrow to represent the image. [3 marks]

b Calculate the magnification of the lens. Use the correct equation from the Physics equations sheet.

Magnification = _____ [2 marks]

c State whether the image is real or virtual.

_____ [1 mark]

A perfect black body

1. An object absorbs all the infrared radiation that falls on it, but transmits gamma rays. Is the object a black body? Give a reason for your answer.

_____ [1 mark]

2. Which is the best possible emitter of radiation? Tick **one** box.

A perfect black body ☐

A shiny surface ☐

A matt black surface ☐ [1 mark]

3. All objects, whatever their temperature, emit and absorb infrared radiation. What can you say about other wavelengths of radiation emitted?

_____ [1 mark]

4. As an object gets hotter, the rate at which it emits radiation increases.

Describe **one** other change to the radiation emitted by the object as its temperature increases.

_____ [1 mark]

5. Explain how a body that is absorbing infrared radiation can be at a constant temperature.

Higher Tier only

_____

_____

_____

_____ [3 marks]

Temperature of the Earth

1. The temperature of any object, including the Earth, is linked to the amount of radiation absorbed and emitted.

Higher Tier only

Complete **Table 3** to state if the temperature of the body increases, decreases or remains the same.

Rate at which object absorbs radiation	Temperature of the object
greater than the rate of emission	
equal to the rate of emission	
less than the rate of emission	

Table 3 [3 marks]

2. The Earth's temperature depends on the balance between the rate of incoming solar radiation, the rate at which this radiation is reflected back into space and the rate at which the Earth's surface and atmosphere absorbs and emits radiation.

Higher Tier only

a The equation gives one possible scenario that alters the radiation balance:

incoming solar radiation > reflected solar radiation + radiation emitted by Earth's surface and atmosphere

State if the temperature of the Earth will increase, decrease or remain the same.

_____ [1 mark]

b Suggest **one** factor that can change the rate at which the Earth's surface reflects radiation back into space.

_____

_____ [1 mark]

c The rate at which radiation is emitted by the Earth's surface and atmosphere depends on how much of the incoming solar radiation is **absorbed**.

State **one** factor that can increase the rate at which incoming solar radiation is absorbed by the atmosphere.

_____

_____ [1 mark]

Magnets and magnetic forces

1. Two bar magnets are placed on a table a short distance apart (**Figure 1**).

| | N | | N | |

Figure 1

Which two statements correctly describe the force between the two north poles of the magnets? Tick **two** boxes.

The force is attractive ☐

The force is repulsive ☐

The force is a contact force ☐

The force is a non-contact force ☐   [2 marks]

2. A student places one end of a permanent magnet into a bag of iron nails. As she removes the magnet from the bag, three nails hang in a chain from the north pole (**Figure 2**). When she moves the top nail away from the magnet, the other two nails separate and fall to the ground.

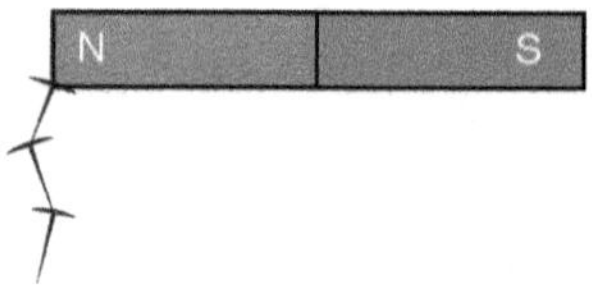

| N | S |

Figure 2

Explain the observations.

_____

_____

_____

_____

_____

_____   [4 marks]

Magnetic fields

1. Which two materials are **not** magnetic materials? Tick **two** boxes.   [2 marks]

Copper ☐   Nickel ☐   Iron ☐   Aluminium ☐   [1 mark]

2. **a** Describe how the direction of a magnetic field at a specific point is defined.

_____

_____ [2 marks]

b The four dotted lines in **Figure 3** represent the magnetic field of the bar magnet. The direction of the field at positions A, B, C and D can be found by placing a small plotting compass at that position.

Figure 3

Draw an arrow on each field line in **Figure 3**, to show the direction that the compass would point at that position.

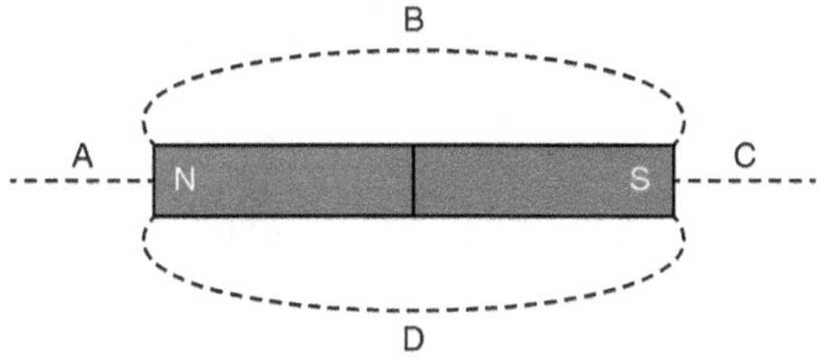

[2 marks]

3. A student suspends a bar magnet so that it is free to rotate (**Figure 4**). What would you expect the student to observe about the direction that the magnet points when it comes to rest?

Give a reason for your answer.

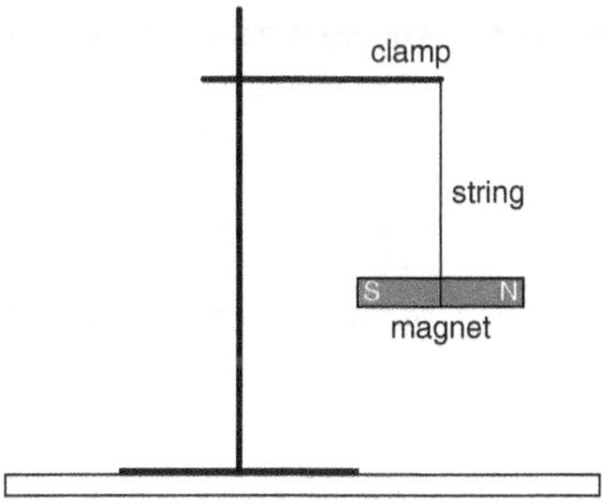

Figure 4

_____

_____

_____

_____ [2 marks]

The magnetic effect of an electric current

1. A wire is clamped vertically through a piece of card (**Figure 5a**). The ends of the wire are connected to a battery (not shown). The current direction though the wire is shown by arrows.

Remember

Use the right-hand grip rule to predict the direction of the magnetic field produced by a straight wire.

a Draw **three** field lines on **Figure 5b** to show the pattern of the magnetic field produced by the current in the wire. Clearly show the direction of the magnetic field. [3 marks]

b A single straight wire, carrying a current, produces a weak magnetic field. Describe how a long wire can be used to produce a strong electromagnet.

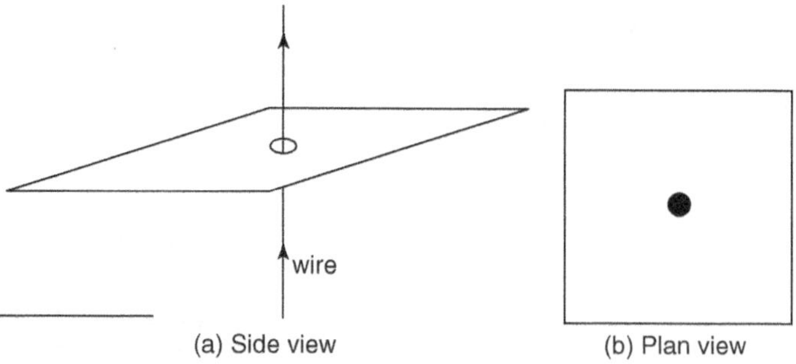

(a) Side view   (b) Plan view

Figure 5

_____

_____

_____

_____ [2 marks]

2. The circuit for an electric door bell is shown in **Figure 6**. The arrows show the direction the current through the wire when the push switch is pressed.

Explain, step by step, how the hammer repeatedly hits the gong while the push switch is being pressed and held down.

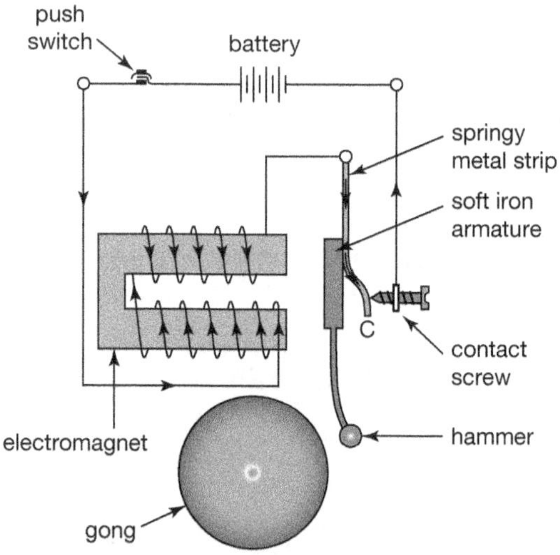

Figure 6

_____

_____

_____

_____

_____

_____

_____

_____

_____

_____ [6 marks]

Fleming's left-hand rule

1.

Higher Tier only

Figure 7 shows a section of a wire carrying a current. The wire is placed in a magnetic field created by two bar magnets.

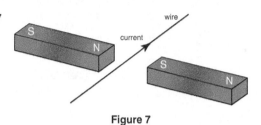

Figure 7

Remember

Use Fleming's left-hand rule to predict the direction of the force on a wire carrying an electric current in a magnetic field.

What is the direction of the magnetic force on the wire? Tick **one** box.

From N to S ☐   Vertically upwards ☐

Vertically downwards ☐   In the direction of the current ☐   [1 mark]

Worked Example

Higher Tier only

The length of wire within a magnetic field is 10 cm. The wire carries a current of 2.0 A. The magnetic flux density of the field is 0.30 T. Calculate the magnetic force on the wire.

Select the correct equation from the Physics equations sheet. [2 marks]

Maths

The equation linking magnetic force to magnetic flux density, current and length is given on the Physics equations sheet. You need to be able to select and apply this equation.

Magnetic force $F = BIL = 0.30 \times 2.0 \times 0.10$ [1 mark]

$= 0.060$ N [1 mark]

2.

Higher Tier only

A magnetic field is created by two slab magnets with opposite poles facing. The direction of the magnetic field is shown by arrows. A wire is placed between the two magnets (**Figure 8**).

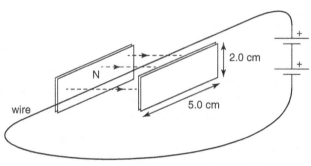

Figure 8

a Determine the direction of the force on the wire.

_____   [1 mark]

Maths Skills

b The dimensions of the magnets are shown on **Figure 8**. The magnetic flux density of the field is 200 mT. The current in the wire is 1.0 A. Determine the size of the magnetic force on the wire.

Select the correct equation from the Physics equations sheet.

Force = _____ N   [3 marks]

c Describe a modification to the apparatus in **Figure 8** that would increase the size of the magnetic force on the wire.

Give a reason for your answer.

_____

_____

_____   [2 marks]

d Describe a modification to the apparatus in **Figure 8** that would reverse the direction of the magnetic force on the wire. Give a reason for your answer.

_____

_____

_____   [2 marks]

Electric motors

1.

Higher Tier only

A simplified diagram of an electric motor is shown in **Figure 9**. The diagram shows a single turn representing the coil of wire. In practice there would be many turns on the coil.

Explain what causes the coil in the electric motor to rotate. Include the function of the split-ring commutator in your explanation.

Remember

In an electric motor, the split-ring commutator makes sure that there is always an upward force on the side of the coil nearest one pole of the magnet and always downwards on the side nearest the other pole.

_____

_____

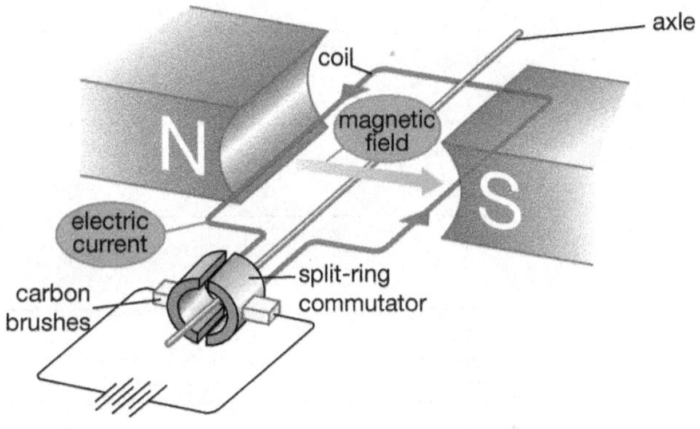

_____

_____

_____

_____

_____

_____

_____

Figure 9

[6 marks]

Loudspeakers

1.

Higher Tier only

Figure 10 shows a side view of the cross-section of a loudspeaker. The diagram shows upper and lower gaps between north and south poles of the magnet.

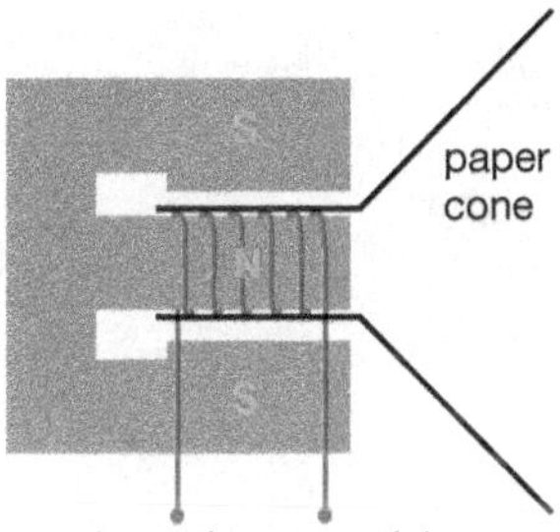

a At one instance, the current in the highest part of the coil in **Figure 10** passes into the page. Use Fleming's left-hand rule to determine the direction of the magnetic force on the coil. Tick **one** box.

Up ☐   Down ☐   Left ☐   Right ☐   [1 mark]

Figure 10

b At the same instant, the current in the lowest part of the coil in **Figure 10** passes out of the page. Use Fleming's left-hand rule to determine the direction of the magnetic force on the lowest part of coil. Tick **one** box.

Up ☐   Down ☐   Left ☐   Right ☐   [1 mark]

c The paper cone and the coil are attached to each other. Explain why the paper cone vibrates if the coil is connected to an alternating potential difference but not if connected to a direct potential difference, such as a battery.

_____

_____

_____

_____

_____

_____

_____

_____

_____ [4 marks]

Induced potential

1.

**Higher
Tier only**

a Explain what is meant by the **generator effect**.

_____

_____

_____ [2 marks]

b State the condition necessary for the generator effect to produce an induced current in a wire.

_____

_____ [1 mark]

2.

**Higher
Tier only**

A length of copper wire is wrapped around a cardboard tube to form a coil (**Figure 11**). The ends of the coil are connected to a digital voltmeter.

a Describe what would be observed when a permanent magnet is moved into the coil, held stationary inside the coil and then moved out of the coil. Explain your answer.

_____

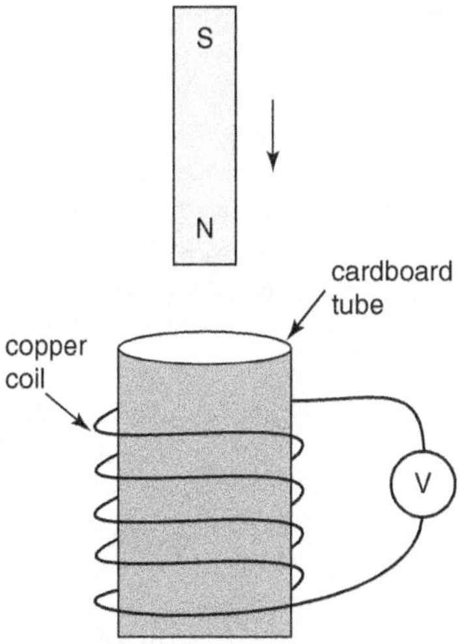

_____

_____

_____

_____

_____

_____

_____

_____

_____

Figure 11

[6 marks]

b The voltmeter in **Figure 11** is now replaced with an ammeter forming a complete circuit. When the magnet is moved slowly into the coil, a maximum current of +10 mA is recorded.

Which current reading is likely to be recorded when the magnet is removed quickly from the coil? Tick **one** box.

–20 mA ☐   –10 mA ☐   0 A ☐   +10 mA ☐   +20 mA ☐

c The current induced in the coil creates its own magnetic field. Describe the effect of the current induced when a magnet is moved **into** the coil.

_____

_____ [1 mark]

d Describe the effect of the induced current created by a magnet being moved **out** of the coil.

_____

_____ [1 mark]

Uses of the generator effect

1. **Figure 12** represents a simplified hand driven a.c. generator also known as an alternator.

Higher Tier only

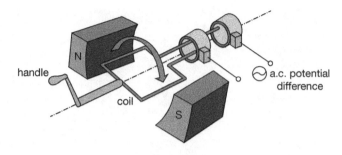

Figure 12

a A student rotates the handle of the alternator. The output from the alternator is shown in **Figure 13**.

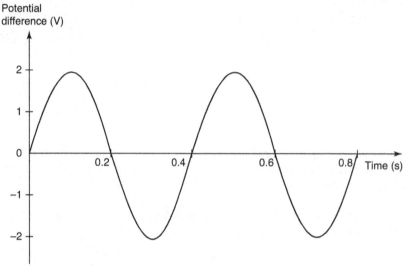

Figure 13

Use **Figure 13** to determine the maximum output potential difference of the alternator.

Maximum output potential difference = _____ V   [1 mark]

b Use **Figure 13** to determine the time for the coil of the alternator to make one complete rotation.

Time = _____ s   [1 mark]

c Determine the number of complete rotations made by the coil in 1 second.

Number of rotations = _____   [1 mark]

d The student now rotates the coil much faster. Describe how this affects the maximum output potential difference and the time for one complete rotation.

Command words

Sketch means to draw approximately using any data supplied in the question.

_____

_____

_____ [2 marks]

2. On the axes in **Figure 14**, sketch the graph of the output potential difference from a d.c. generator versus time. The maximum output voltage is 5V and the time for one complete

Higher Tier only rotation of the generator's coil is 0.10 s. [3 marks]

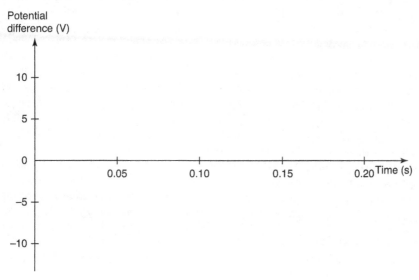

Figure 14

Microphones

1. **Figure 15** shows a moving coil microphone.

Higher Tier only

a The incoming sound wave makes the flexible diaphragm of the microphone vibrate. Describe how this vibration produces an output potential difference.

_____

_____

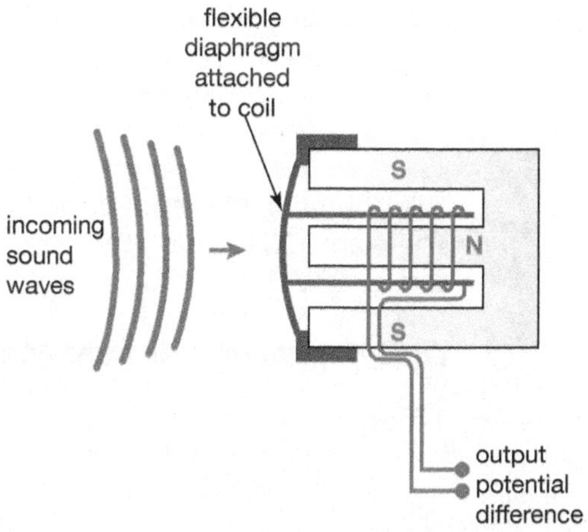

Figure 15

_____

_____

_____ [3 marks]

b Give the name of the effect given to the production of a potential difference by the microphone.

_____ [1 mark]

c What type of potential difference is produced by the microphone?

_____ [1 mark]

Transformers

Worked Example A school laboratory power supply unit contains a transformer with a 600 turn primary coil. Calculate the number of turns on the secondary when the supply unit is plugged into the 230 V mains and provides a 6.0 V output potential difference.

Give your answer as a whole number. [4 marks]

Maths
You need to be able to select and apply the two transformer equations: $\frac{V_p}{V_s} = \frac{n_p}{n_s}$ and $V_s I_s = V_p I_p$ from the Physics equations sheet.

Use $\frac{V_p}{V_s} = \frac{n_p}{n_s}$

$\frac{230}{6.0} = \frac{600}{n_s}$ [1 mark]

Rearranging gives $n_s = \frac{600 \times 6.0}{230}$ [1 mark]

$= 15.6$ [1 mark], round to 16 [1 mark]

1. The potential difference applied to the primary coil of an industrial transformer is 420 V. There are 400 turns on the primary coil. The output potential difference from the secondary coil is 100 V.

What is the number of turns on the secondary coil? Tick **one** box.

1700 ☐   95 ☐   170 ☐   950 ☐   [1 mark]

2.

Higher
Tier only

Figure 16 represents a transformer used to transfer energy from the mains to a toy train set.

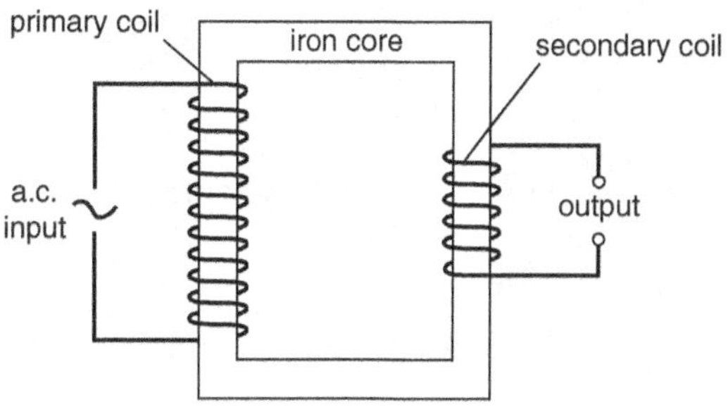

Figure 16

a State what type of transformer is shown in **Figure 16**.

_____ [1 mark]

b State why iron is a suitable material for the core of the transformer.

_____ [1 mark]

c The toy train set requires a 12 V power supply. The transformer used to transfer energy to the train set from the 230 V mains has a 500 turn primary coil.

Calculate the number of turns on its secondary coil. Give your answer as a whole number.

Select the correct equation from the Physics equations sheet.

Number of turns = _____ [4 marks]

d The current in the primary coil is 0.40 A. Calculate the current induced in the secondary coil assuming that the transformer is 100% efficient. Give your answer to 2 significant figures.

Select the correct equation from the Physics equations sheet.

Current = _____ A [4 marks]

e Explain why the primary coil of a transformer must be connected to an alternating p.d. and not to a battery for the transformer to work.

Synoptic

In the final exam some marks will be given for connecting knowledge from different physics topics.

_____

_____

_____

_____ [3 marks]

125

3. A school power supply unit contains a transformer. A student uses the power supply unit to supply a 12V potential difference to a lamp. She plugs the power supply unit into the 230V mains.

Synoptic **a** Calculate the current flowing through the lamp if the power dissipated by the lamp is 24W.

Current = _____ A   [3 marks]

b Assuming that the transformer inside the power supply unit is 100% efficient, calculate the current flowing in the primary coil of the transformer. Give your answer to 2 significant figures.

Select the correct equation from the Physics equations sheet.

Current = _____ A   [4 marks]

Synoptic **c** After a while, the student observes that the power supply unit gets warm. Suggest an explanation for this observation.

_____

_____   [2 marks]

Our Solar System

....

1. The main objects in the Solar System include the Sun, planets and moons. Describe how these bodies move in relation to each other.

    _____

    _____

    _____ [2 marks]

2. The closest astronomical object to the Earth is the Moon at 3.85×10^5 km. The next closest object is the planet Venus. The closest Venus approaches the Earth is 38 million km.

    Maths Skills

    Maths

    Orders of magnitude can be used to make an approximate comparison of two distances. For example, a distance that is approximately 1000 times greater than another is 3 orders of magnitude greater. Note that the order of magnitude is equal to the number of zeroes.

    a   Determine approximately how many times further away Venus is than the Moon.

    Number of times = _____ [1 mark]

    b   Determine how many orders of magnitude greater the Earth–Venus distance is compared with the Earth–Moon distance.

    Number of orders of magnitude = _____ [1 mark]

3. a   Describe how the Sun was formed.

    _____

    _____ [2 marks]

    Synoptic   b   The Sun radiates a huge amount of energy every second. Describe how the Sun generates this energy.

    _____

    _____

    _____

    _____ [4 marks]

The life cycle of a star

1. **a** In about 5 billion years the Sun will no longer be a main sequence star and will enter the next stage in its life. Complete **Figure 1** to show the future stages in the life of the Sun.

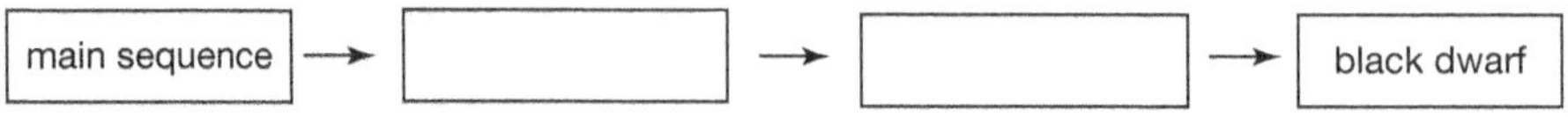

| main sequence | → | [ ] | → | [ ] | → | black dwarf |

Figure 1 [2 marks]

b Betelgeuse is a star currently in its red supergiant stage. It is many times more massive than the Sun. Complete **Figure 2** to show the possible future stages in the life of Betelgeuse.

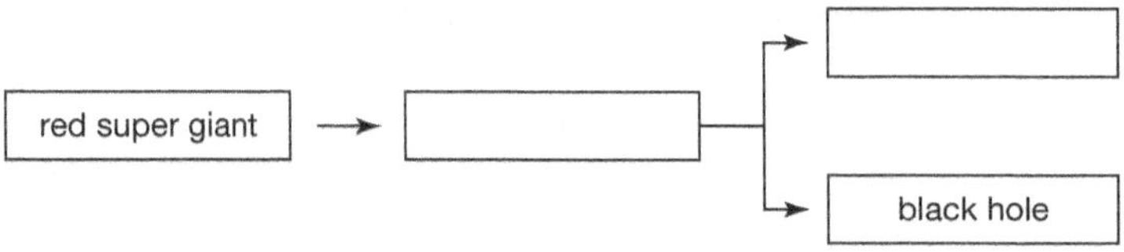

red super giant → [ ] → [ ]
                              [ ]
                              black hole

Figure 2 [2 marks]

2. Iron is the heaviest element that can be produced by nuclear fusion inside a star. Describe how elements heavier than iron are produced and distributed throughout a galaxy.

_____

_____

_____

_____

_____ [4 marks]

Orbital motion, natural and artificial satellites

1. The speed against distance graph for seven planets in orbit around the Sun is shown in **Figure 3**.

Maths Skills

a Draw a line of best fit through the points in **Figure 3**. [1 mark]

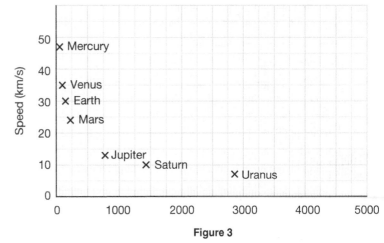

Figure 3

b State what **Figure 3** shows about the relation between a planet's orbital speed and its distance from the Sun.

_____ [1 mark]

c The planet Neptune orbits the Sun at a distance of about 4500 million km. Use **Figure 3** to predict Neptune's orbital speed.

Speed = _____ km/s [1 mark]

d Describe the main difference between a planet and a moon.

_____

_____ [2 marks]

e The circumference of the Moon's orbit around the Earth is 2.4×10^6 km. The Moon completes one orbit in 27 days.

Calculate the Moon's orbital speed. Give your answer in km/s to 2 significant figures.

Maths

Don't forget to convert units: there are 24 hours in one day; 60 minutes in one hour; 60 seconds in one minute.

Speed = _____ km/s [5 marks]

2. The altitude of an artificial satellite's orbit is chosen depending on the purpose of the satellite. Many of NASA's EOS satellites used for observing the land and the oceans are put into a low orbit at an altitude of about 800 km.

For these satellites to maintain a stable orbit, they must have an orbital speed of 7.5 km/s.

a What would happen to the satellite if its speed was lower than 7.5 km/s?

_____ [1 mark]

b What would happen to the satellite if its speed was higher than 7.5 km/s?

_____ [1 mark]

Maths Skills

c An EOS satellite orbits the Earth every 100 minutes. How many complete orbits does it make in one day?

Give your answer as a whole number.

Number of orbits = _____ [3 marks]

d Suggest **one** reason why a satellite making observations of the Earth's surface needs to be in a low orbit rather than in an orbit at a much greater distance from the Earth.

_____ [1 mark]

Red-shift

1. **a** In the early 20th century, astronomers observed that light from distant galaxies was red-shifted. Explain what is meant by **red-shift**.

_____

_____

_____ [3 marks]

b State what can be determined about a distant galaxy from the amount of red-shift that occurs.

_____ [1 mark]

2.

a By 1929 astronomers had enough data to be able to plot a graph of speed against distance for distant galaxies (**Figure 4**).

State what conclusion about distant galaxies can be made from the graph in **Figure 4**.

Explain your answer.

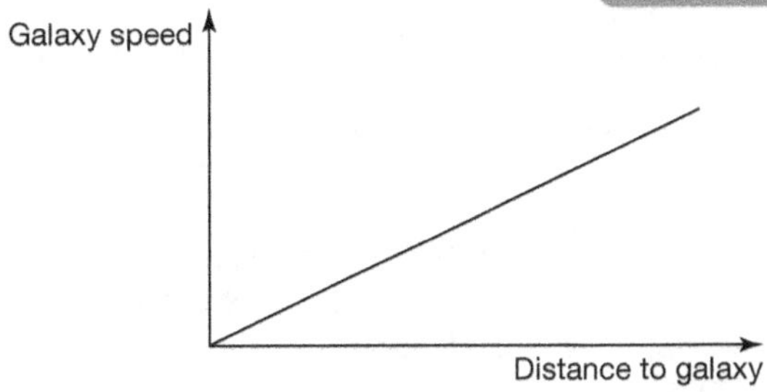

Figure 4

_____

_____

_____ [2 marks]

b Describe the Big Bang theory of the universe. Explain how the graph in **Figure 4** supports the theory.

_____

_____

_____

_____ [4 marks]

c During the 20th century, scientists have made more discoveries that also support the Big Bang theory.

State why it is necessary to search for more evidence to support a scientific theory.

_____

_____ [1 mark]

Dark matter and dark energy

1.

Maths Skills

An estimate of the observed mass in the Milky Way galaxy is 1×10^{42} kg. Estimate the number of stars in the Milky Way if a typical star has a mass of 5×10^{30} kg.

Give your answer in billions where 1 billion = 1×10^9.

Maths

You need to be able to convert numbers written in standard form to other forms. For example, $5 \times 10^{12} = 5000 \times 10^9$, so this is 5000 billion.

Number of stars = _____ billion

[3 marks]

2. The stars in nearby spiral galaxies are observed to orbit around the centre of the galaxy.

Curve **X** in **Figure 5** shows how the speed of stars varies with their distance from the centre of a galaxy. Curve **X** is based on actual speed measurements of stars in the galaxy.

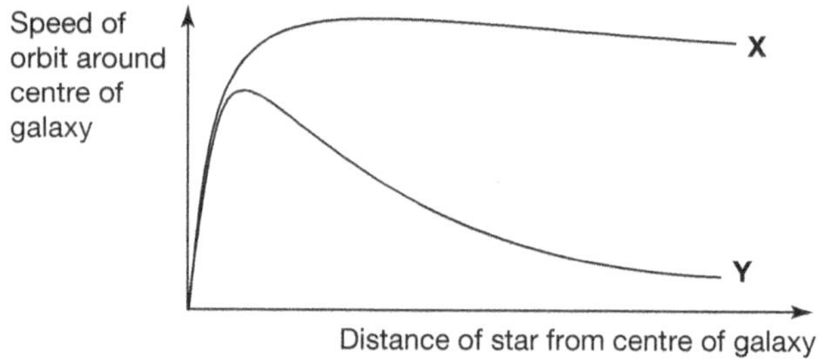

Curve **Y** is a theoretical prediction based on the mass that can be observed in a galaxy and what is known about the force of gravity.

Figure 5

Maths Skills

a Compare the trends in star speed shown by curves **X** and **Y**.

Remember

In a **compare** question you need to give both similarities and differences.

_____

_____

_____

_____ [3 marks]

b Some scientists had the idea that the differences between curve **X** and curve **Y** can be explained if there is more mass in the galaxy than be observed directly.

State the name given to this 'invisible' mass. _____ [1 mark]

c Suggest what evidence would be needed to support the idea proposed in part (b).

_____ [1 mark]

d Scientists have made observations that suggest that the expansion of the universe is accelerating. State the name of the concept introduced to try to explain this observation.

_____ [1 mark]

Physics equation sheet

It is important to be able to recall and apply the following equations using standard units:

Equation Number	Word Equation	Symbol Equation
1	weight = mass × gravitational field strength	$W = mg$
2	work done = force × distance (along the line of action of the force)	$W = Fs$
3	force applied to a spring = spring constant × extension	$F = ke$
4	moment of a force = force × distance (normal to direction of force)	$M = Fd$
5	pressure = $\dfrac{\text{force normal to a surface}}{\text{area of that surface}}$	$p = \dfrac{F}{A}$
6	distance travelled = speed × time	$s = vt$
7	acceleration = $\dfrac{\text{change in velocity}}{\text{time taken}}$	$a = \dfrac{\Delta v}{t}$
8	resultant force = mass × acceleration	$F = ma$
9	momentum = mass × velocity	$p = mv$
10	kinetic energy = 0.5 × mass × (speed)²	$E_k = \frac{1}{2}mv^2$
11	gravitational potential energy = mass × gravitational field strength × height	$E_p = mgh$
12	power = $\dfrac{\text{energy transferred}}{\text{time}}$	$P = \dfrac{E}{t}$
13	power = $\dfrac{\text{work done}}{\text{time}}$	$P = \dfrac{W}{t}$
14	efficiency = $\dfrac{\text{useful output energy transfer}}{\text{useful input energy transfer}}$	
15	efficiency = $\dfrac{\text{useful power output}}{\text{total power input}}$	
16	wave speed = frequency × wavelength	$v = f\lambda$
17	charge flow = current × time	$Q = It$
18	potential difference = current × resistance	$V = IR$
19	power = potential difference × current	$P = VI$
20	power = (current)² × resistance	$P = I^2R$

Equation Number	Word Equation	Symbol Equation
21	energy transferred = power × time	$E = Pt$
22	energy transferred = charge flow × potential difference	$E = QV$
23	density = $\dfrac{\text{mass}}{\text{volume}}$	$\rho = \dfrac{m}{V}$

The following equations will appear on the equations sheet that you are given in the exam. It is important to be able to select and apply the appropriate equation to answer a question correctly.

Equation Number	Word Equation	Symbol Equation
1	pressure due to a column of liquid = height of column × density of liquid × gravitational field strength	$p = h\rho g$
2	(final velocity)² − (initial velocity)² = 2 × acceleration × distance	$v^2 - u^2 = 2as$
3	force = $\dfrac{\text{change in momentum}}{\text{time taken}}$	$F = \dfrac{m\Delta v}{\Delta t}$
4	elastic potential energy = 0.5 × spring constant × (extension)²	$E_e = \frac{1}{2}ke^2$
5	change in thermal energy = mass × specific heat capacity × temperature change	$\Delta E = mc\Delta\theta$
6	magnification = $\dfrac{\text{image height}}{\text{object height}}$	
7	period = $\dfrac{1}{\text{frequency}}$	
8	force on a conductor (at right-angles to a magnetic field) = magnetic flux density × current × length	$F = BIl$
9	thermal energy for a change of state = mass × specific latent heat	$E = mL$
10	$\dfrac{\text{potential difference across primary coil}}{\text{potential difference across secondary coil}} = \dfrac{\text{number of turns in primary coil}}{\text{number of turns in secondary coil}}$	$\dfrac{V_p}{V_s} = \dfrac{n_p}{n_s}$
11	potential difference across primary coil × current in primary coil = potential difference across secondary coil × current in secondary coil	$V_p I_p = V_s I_s$
12	For gases: pressure × volume = constant	$pV = \text{constant}$

Section 1: Energy changes in a system

Energy stores and systems

1. Thermal energy store of the system. [1 mark]

2. a The moving vehicle has a store of kinetic energy. [1 mark] When the vehicle slows down the store of kinetic energy decreases [1 mark]; the store of thermal energy (in the surrounding air/brakes) increases. [1 mark]

   b The stationary vehicle has a store of thermal energy (in hot brakes/engine). [1 mark] Thermal energy store in hot brakes and hot engine decreases [1 mark]; thermal energy store in surrounding air increases. [1 mark]

3. Energy is transferred by motor to the drum/force transfers energy to the drum by doing work [1 mark]; energy transferred by heating/electrical work to water in clothes [1 mark]; kinetic energy store of the (rotating) drum increases [1 mark]; internal (thermal) energy store of water in clothes increases. [1 mark]

Calculating energy changes

1. Extension = 0.3 m [1 mark]; elastic potential energy = $0.5 \times 5.0 \times 0.3^2$ [1 mark]; 0.23 J [1 mark]

2. $0.18 = 0.5 \times 36 \times e^2$ [1 mark]; $e = \sqrt{\frac{2 \times 0.18}{36}}$ [1 mark]; 0.10 m [1 mark]

3. a Kinetic energy = $\frac{1}{2}mv^2$ [1 mark] accept word equation: kinetic energy = 0.5 × mass × (speed)^2

   b Kinetic energy = $0.5 \times 2000 \times 12^2$ [1 mark]
   144 000 J [1 mark]
   144 kJ [1 mark]

   c Kinetic energy at 20 m/s = $0.5 \times 2000 \times 20^2$ [1 mark]; 400 000 J or 400 kJ [1 mark]; increase in kinetic energy = (400 − 144) kJ = 256 kJ [1 mark]

4. a Gravitational potential energy = $40 \times 9.8 \times 25$ [1 mark]; 9800 J [1 mark]

   b Kinetic energy gained = 0.5×9800 J [1 mark]; 4900 J [1 mark]; $0.5 \times 40 \times v^2 = 4900$ [1 mark] $v = \sqrt{\frac{2 \times 4900}{40}}$ or $\sqrt{245}$ [1 mark] = 15.65248 m/s [1 mark] 16 m/s (2 significant figures) [1 mark]

Calculating energy changes when a system is heated

1. Temperature change = 100 − 20 = 80°C [1 mark]; $\Delta E = 0.75 \times 4200 \times 80$ [1 mark] = 252 000 J [1 mark]

2. $36000 = 0.2 \times 2200 \times \Delta\theta$ [1 mark]; $\Delta\theta = \frac{36000}{0.2 \times 2200}$ [1 mark] = 81.81 °C [1 mark] 82°C (2 significant figures) [1 mark]

3. a $\Delta E = 50 \times (10 \times 60)$ [1 mark] = 30 000 J [1 mark]

   b Electronic balance [1 mark]; thermometer [1 mark]

   c The marks are in two bands according to the level of response.

Level 2 (3/4): The method is described in detail and could be followed by someone else to obtain valid results.
Level 1 (1/2): Simple statements are made about some of the relevant parts of the method but the steps may not be in an order that makes sense and may not lead to the production of valid results.
0: No relevant content
Indicative content: • Measure the mass of the block with the electronic balance. • Place thermometer in hole in (or in contact with) the steel block. • Measure the temperature and switch on the stop clock. • Measure the change in temperature (of the block) over 10 minutes. • Calculate specific heat capacity using: change in thermal energy = mass × specific heat capacity × temperature change. • Measurements repeated at least once to spot anomalies/continue heating and measure temperature change for at least one more 10 minute interval. • Use repeats (ignore anomalies) to calculate the mean value.

   d The block is not insulated [1 mark] so heater will have to supply more energy to make the temperature of the block rise (by 1 °C)/some of the energy transferred by the heater to the block is transferred to the surrounding air and does not make the temperature of the block rise. [1 mark] *or* There is air between the heater and the metal block [1 mark] so some of the energy transferred from the heater is transferred to the air rather than to the steel block. [1 mark]

Work and power

1. watt/W (do not accept J/s) [1 mark]
2. Half as long [1 mark]
3. Energy transferred = $20 \times (2 \times 60 \times 60)$ [1 mark] = 144 000 J [1 mark]
4. Increase in kinetic energy = $0.5 \times 1200 \times (15)^2$ [1 mark] = 135 000 J [1 mark]; power = $\frac{135\,000}{10}$ [1 mark] = 13 500 W [1 mark]
5. Increase in gravitational potential energy = $1050 \times 9.8 \times 196$ [1 mark] = 2 016 840 J [1 mark]; power = $\frac{2\,016\,840}{38}$ [1 mark] = 53 075 W [1 mark] 53 000 W (2 significant figures) [1 mark]

Conservation of energy

1. Dissipated/transferred to (thermal energy store of) the surroundings. [1 mark]
2. Not all of the energy is transferred from the kinetic energy store of the air to the wind turbine [1 mark] Some energy is dissipated (or 'wasted') to the thermal energy store of the surroundings (due to friction and/or air resistance and/or electrical heating in the generator). [1 mark] There is no net change to the total energy/for every 500 J of input energy, 380 J is transferred to the surroundings. [1 mark]
3. The marks are in two bands according to the level of response.

Level 2 (3/4): A detailed explanation with logical links between clearly identified relevant points.
Level 1 (1/2): Relevant, but separate, points are made. The logic may be unclear.
0: No relevant content

Indicative content:

- The kinetic energy store of the cyclist and her bike decreases.
- Energy is transferred away from the bike because work is done by friction.
- Energy is dissipated to the surroundings by heating/thermal energy store of the surroundings increases.

- The total energy of the system (the cyclist, her bike and the surroundings) is constant.
- Decrease in kinetic energy store of cyclist and her bike equals increase in thermal energy store of the surroundings/no net change to the total energy of the system.

4. Gravitational potential energy gained = $0.450 \times 9.8 \times 2.3 = 10.143$ J [1 mark]; kinetic energy gained when ball loses this amount of GPE = 10.143 J [1 mark]; $10.143 = 0.5 \times 0.450 \times v^2$ [1 mark]; $v = \sqrt{\frac{2 \times 10.143}{0.450}}$ or $\sqrt{45.08}$ [1 mark] = 6.714 m/s [1 mark] 6.7 m/s (2 significant figures) [1 mark]

Ways of reducing unwanted energy transfers

1. **a** Decrease in thermal energy stored in building causes temperature to fall [1 mark], so more fuel/electricity needed to heat building to keep temperature same. [1 mark]
   b The higher the thermal conductivity the higher the rate of energy transfer across the material. [1 mark]
   c Low [1 mark] because reduces the rate at which thermal energy stored in the building moves out of the building. [1 mark]
2. Lubrication/oil reduces friction between the moving parts [1 mark]; (work done by) friction dissipates energy to the surroundings [1 mark]; so less friction means less work must be done to turn the cube. [1 mark]
3. **a** To control volume of hot water [1 mark]; to make it a valid comparison [1 mark]
   b Curves (concave) not straight lines [1 mark]; both curves start at same temperature [1 mark]; curve labelled good insulator is flatter/stays at higher temperature for longer. [1 mark]

Efficiency

1. Efficiency = (useful output energy transfer) ÷ (total input energy transfer) [1 mark]
2. The useful output energy is only 40% of the total input energy/only 40% of the total input energy is transferred to useful output energy/60% of the energy is wasted [1 mark]

3. a $\Delta E = 0.9 \times 4200 \times (98 - 18)$ [1 mark];
302 400 J [1 mark]

b Efficiency $= \frac{302\,400}{420\,000}$ [1 mark]; 0.72 [1 mark]
(no mark if % sign on end) or 72% [1 mark]
(no mark if % sign not added)

c One of: use a lid on the pan/increase area of pan in contact with the hob/use an electric kettle with a plastic body. [1 mark]

Because some of the thermal energy transferred by the hob heats the pan/ some of the thermal energy passes into air because some areas of the hob are not in contact with the pan/heated water transfers thermal energy to the air above it/plastic is an insulator and reduces energy losses to the surroundings. [1 mark]

If more of the input energy is used usefully (to heat the water) this will increase the efficiency [1 mark]

4. One of: use the heated water (cooling water) to heat nearby buildings/find a way of using the energy transferred by heating that would otherwise be wasted [1 mark]

If more of the input energy is used usefully this will increase the efficiency [1 mark]

National and global energy resources

1. Biofuels can be used for heating, the others cannot. [1 mark]

2. Any two of: coal/oil/gas/fossil fuels creates atmospheric pollution/particulates which cause health problems/acid rain; fossil fuels produce carbon dioxide when burned, so contribute to climate change; non-renewable fuels will eventually run out/ not replenished (ignore any reference to nuclear power). [1 mark each]

3. a Gas: Initially only small changes/no trend, then sudden, large increase from 2015 to 2016. [1 mark] Percentage of electricity generated by renewables increased, but by a much smaller amount than for gas. [1 mark]

b The share of electricity generated from gas rose as an alternative to coal fired generation/people are more environmentally aware and are switching to green sources of electricity. [1 mark]

4 Nuclear power station is reliable because it produces a constant power output. [1 mark]

Wind turbines don't generate power if the wind is not blowing so not reliable. [1 mark]

5 The marks are in two bands according to the level of response.

Level 2 (3/4): A clear coherent description with valid comparisons and logical links between relevant points.
Level 1 (1/2): Some relevant points made, direct comparisons may not be made.
0: No relevant content

Indicative content:
- Use of wind turbines does not directly result in carbon dioxide emissions/does not directly cause climate change.
- However during manufacture of components for a wind turbine fossil fuel resources will be used.
  * No pollutant gases/particles produced during operation of either, but some pollution produced during manufacture of component parts (for both).
- Use of nuclear fuel does not directly result in carbon dioxide emissions.
- However during building of a nuclear power station fossil fuel resources will be used.
- Use of nuclear fuel produces radioactive waste.
- Radioactive waste will be hazardous for hundreds of years.
  * Must be treated and stored somehow.
  * No radioactive waste produced from a wind turbine.
- Wind turbines may be considered to cause visual pollution.
- Noise pollution from wind turbines
  * No noise pollution from a nuclear power station.

Section 2: Electricity

Circuit diagrams

1. 1 mark for each correctly named symbol:

symbol	+ ⊢	+ ⊢---⊢	⎓	☀
name	cell	battery	thermistor	LDR/light dependent resistor

2. 1 mark for each correctly drawn symbol:

symbol	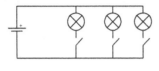		
name	fixed resistor	variable resistor	ammeter

3. Cell and three lamps connected as shown in diagram. [1 mark] Three switches as shown. [1 mark]

Electrical charge and current

1. a $Q = I\,t$ [1 mark] (accept word equation: charge flow = current × time)

  b $Q = 0.020 \times 100$ [1 mark] = 2.0 C [1 mark]

  c $1.2 = I \times 100$ [1 mark] $I = \frac{1.2}{100}$ [1 mark] = 0.012 A [1 mark] = 12 mA [1 mark]

2. Conversion of 200 µA to 200×10^{-6} A [1 mark]; $1 = 200 \times 10^{-6} \times t$ [1 mark]; $t = \frac{1}{200 \times 10^{-6}}$ [1 mark] = 5000 s [1 mark]

Electrical resistance

1. $9.0 = I \times 200$ [1 mark]; $I = \frac{9.0}{200}$ [1 mark] = 0.045 A [1 mark] = 45 mA [1 mark]

2. Conversion of 60 mA to 0.060 A [1 mark]; $1.5 = 0.060 \times R$ [1 mark] $= R = \frac{1.5}{0.060}$ [1 mark] = 25 Ω [1 mark]

3. a Circuit diagram to include a cell/battery/power supply unit as shown in diagram. [1 mark] Ammeter in the correct position. [1 mark] Voltmeter in the correct position. [1 mark]

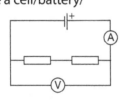

  b Resistance is found by dividing the voltmeter reading by ammeter reading [2 marks] (but give 1 mark for potential difference divided by current).

4. a The diameter will affect the wire's resistance [1 mark] Either: only want the change in length to affect the resistance, or need to control variables other than length for [1 mark]

  b Any kinks would result in the length measurement being incorrect (or could change the thickness) [1 mark]

c Dependent variable: resistance. [1 mark] Independent variable: length. [1 mark] Control variable: diameter. [1 mark] Allow type of wire [1 mark]

d 0.1 m to 0.8 m [1 mark]

e Straight line through the origin [1 mark]

f 0.24 (m) [1 mark]

g Accept in the range of 6.5 to 7.0 Ω/m [1 mark]

Resistors and I–V characteristics

1. a P: thermistor [1 mark] Q: light dependent resistor (accept LDR) [1 mark]

  b Increase temperature [1 mark]

  c Decrease the brightness/intensity of the light [1 mark]

  d Component P [1 mark]

2. a Straight line through the origin [1 mark]

  b Accept any of the following for 1 mark: Ohmic conductor; fixed resistor, constant/fixed resistance allows current to flow in either direction.

3. a C [1 mark]

  b B [1 mark]

4. a Cell/battery/power supply. [1 mark] Complete circuit (see diagram below) with ammeter and voltmeter in correct positions [1 mark]; either variable resistor in suitable position to change current/p.d. in the circuit or variable power supply. [1 mark]

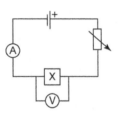

  b The marks are in three bands according to the level of response:

Level 3 (5/6 marks): A detailed and coherent plan, with steps presented in a logical sequence, that would produce sufficient data to enable an I-V characteristic graph (including both positive and negative data) to be plotted. Some valid suggestions about reducing errors are made, with reasons.

Level 2 (3/4 marks): A plan that would produce a valid set of current and potential difference data. The method may not be in a completely logical sequence and may be missing some detail.

Level 1 (1/2 marks): Some relevant comments but the plan would not enable another person to obtain valid results. The answer may lack a logical structure, or give no indication of what to do with the results.

0: No relevant content

Indicative content:

- Current measured with ammeter.
- P.d. measured with voltmeter.
- Measurements repeated at least twice at this setting to spot anomalies.
- Variable resistor (or variable power supply) adjusted so that another set of current and p.d. readings can be taken, and repeated at least twice.
- Voltage should not be allowed to get so high as to damage the component/ change its temperature
- Disconnect the battery between readings to avoid overheating
- Process repeated to obtain at least 6 sets of current and p.d. readings.
- Use repeats (ignore anomalies) to obtain mean current and p.d. values (to reduce effect of random errors).
- Connections to the cell/battery (swap the leads at the power supply) are reversed.
- Process repeated to obtain at least 6 *negative* p.d. values.
- Plot a graph of current (y axis) against p.d. (x axis)

Series and parallel circuits

1. (Open switch) total resistance = 40 + 60 = 100 Ω [1 mark]; 6.0 = I × 100 [1 mark]; ammeter reading $I = \frac{6.0}{100}$ [1 mark] = 0.060 A [1 mark]

   (Closed switch) ammeter reading = $\frac{6.0}{60}$ [1 mark] = 0.10 A [1 mark]

2. **a** Resistance = 1400 + 600 = 2000 Ω [1 mark]

b 12 = I × 2000 [1 mark] Ammeter reading = I = $\frac{12}{2000}$ [1 mark] = 0.0060 A [1 mark] = 6.0 mA [1 mark]

c Voltmeter reading = IR = 0.0060 × 1400 [1 mark] = 8.4 V [1 mark]

d Resistance of LDR/component X increases. [1 mark] Current decreases. [1 mark] Potential difference across the fixed resistor decreases [1 mark] so voltmeter reading decreases. [1 mark] Alternative answer: Resistance of LDR/component X increases [1 mark] making resistance of component Y a smaller fraction of the total circuit resistance. [1 mark] Hence smaller p.d. across Y [1 mark] so voltmeter reading decreases. [1 mark]

3. The potential difference across each of the resistors has the same value. [1 mark] The current through each of the resistors has a different value. [1 mark]

4. **a** 6.0 V [1 mark]

   b 6.0 = I × 20 [1 mark]; current = $\frac{6.0}{20}$ [1 mark] = 0.30 A [1 mark]

   c Current = 2 × 0.30 = 0.60 A [1 mark]

Mains electricity

1. An alternating p.d. keeps reversing/changing direction (can have positive or negative values). [1 mark] A direct p.d. does not change direction. [1 mark]

2. 230 V   50 Hz [1 mark]

3. **a** Live wire carries the potential difference from the mains to the appliance. [1 mark] Neutral wire completes the circuit. [1 mark]

   b Earth wire is connected to the metal casing. [1 mark] If the live wire touches the casing, current flows along earth wire [1 mark], blowing the fuse [1 mark] and disconnecting the appliance from the mains. [1 mark]

Energy changes in circuits

1. Conversion of 1.0 kW to 1000 W [1 mark] Energy transferred = 10 000 × 15 × 60 [1 mark] = 900 000 J [1 mark]

2. Conversion of 2.0 kW to 2000 W [1 mark]; energy transferred = 2000 × 60 × 60 [1 mark] = 7 200 000 [1 mark] = 7.2×10^6 J [1 mark]

3. a (Energy from the mains) transferred to the thermal energy store of the heater and surroundings. [1 mark]

b Energy transferred = $Q V = 16\,000 \times 230$ [1 mark] = $3\,680\,000$ [1 mark] = 3.7×10^6 J (2 significant figures, standard form) [1 mark]

4. a Energy transferred = $P t = 2.0 \times 15$ [1 mark] = 30 J [1 mark]

b $E = Q V$, = Rearrange equation to $30 = Q \times 3.0$ [1 mark]; $Q = \frac{30}{3.0}$ [1 mark] = 10 C [1 mark]

Electrical power

1. Conversion of 1.2 kW to 1200 W [1 mark]; $P = V I$, $1200 = 230 \times I$ [1 mark]; $I = \frac{1200}{230}$ [1 mark] 5.21(7391) [1 mark] 5.2 A (2 significant figures) [1 mark]

2. a $P = V I$, $460 = 230 \times I$. [1 mark] Current $I = \frac{460}{230}$ [1 mark] = 2.0 A [1 mark]

b $V = I R$, $230 = 2 \times R$. [1 mark] Resistance $R = \frac{230}{2}$ [1 mark] = 115 Ω. [1 mark]

3. Power = $I^2 R = (0.20)^2 \times 0.3$ [1 mark] = 0.012 W. [1 mark]

4. a Conversion of 2.0 mA to 0.002 A and conversion of 4.0 kΩ to 4000 Ω [1 mark] Power = $(0.002)^2 \times 4000$ [1 mark] = 0.016 W [1 mark]

b Energy transferred = $0.016 \times 5 \times 60$ [1 mark] = 4.8 J [1 mark]

The National Grid

1. a If the supply from a local power station failed then the house would have no electricity. [1 mark] If the house is connected to the National Grid, then there are many power stations that can supply electricity to the house. [1 mark]

b A step-up transformer increases potential difference and a step-down transformer decreases potential difference. [1 mark]

2. a Power = $I^2 R = (30)^2 \times 100$ [1 mark] = 90 000 W [1 mark]

b If the current is smaller, less power is transferred to the surroundings (as heat). [1 mark] So more power is available to consumers/so power is transmitted more efficiently. [1 mark]

c The step-down transformer reduces the potential difference to a much lower level, which is safer for use by consumers. [1 mark]

Static electricity

1. a Electrons are transferred from the cloth [1 mark] to the polythene rod [1 mark]

b There is an attractive force between a positive and a negative charge [1 mark] showing the acetate rod has a positive/an opposite charge. [1 mark]

Electric fields

1. a Place a charged object near to the object and see if it experiences a force. [1 mark]

b Radial pattern [1 mark] arrows radiating outwards [1 mark].

c Force is repulsive [1 mark] force gets bigger (as spheres are pushed together). [1 mark]

Section 3: Particle model of matter

Density

1. a Density = $m/V = \frac{61.2}{4.5}$ [1 mark] = 13.6 [1 mark] g/cm^3 [1 mark]

b Density = m/V, $13.6 = 54.5/\text{volume}$ [1 mark] (allow ecf from part a); volume = $\frac{54.5}{13.6}$ [1 mark] 4(.007) cm^3 [1 mark] 4.0 (2 significant figures) [1 mark]

2. Volume = $25.00 \times 8.50 \times 1.20 = 255$ m^3 [1 mark]; Density = m/V, $1000 = \text{mass}/255$ [1 mark]; mass = 1000×255 [1 mark] = 255 000 kg [1 mark]

3. 789 kg/m^3 = 0.789 g/cm^3 [1 mark]; Density = m/V, $0.789 = \text{mass}/200$ [1 mark]; mass = 0.789×200 [1 mark] = 157.8 g [1 mark] *or* 200 cm^3 = 0.0002 m^3 [1 mark]; $789 = \text{mass}/0.0002$ [1 mark]; mass = 0.789×0.0002 [1 mark] = 0.1578 kg or 157.8 g [1 mark]

4. Density = m/V, 0.92 = 255/volume [1 mark]; volume = $\frac{255}{0.92}$ [1 mark] = 277.17 cm³ [1 mark] 280 cm³ (2 significant figures) [1 mark]

5. The marks are in two bands according to the level of response.

Level 2 (3/4): The method is described in detail and could be followed by someone else to obtain valid results.
Level 1 (1/2): Simple statements are made about some of the relevant parts of the method but the steps may not be in an order that makes sense and may not lead to the production of valid results.
0: No relevant content

Indicative content:
- Fill displacement can with water until it comes up to the spout.
- Submerge pebble in water.
- Measure volume of water displaced/collected in the measuring cylinder.
- Volume of water displaced = volume of pebble.
- Uncertainty in volume = 1 cm³ because the measuring cylinder has smallest scale divisions of 2 cm³ and the scale could be read to the nearest half division.

6. increases [1 mark] because the particles in seawater get further apart. [1 mark]

Changes of state

1. a Sublimation [1 mark]
   b Cool down [1 mark]; iodine gas would desublimate/turn back into solid iodine/same substance/regains its original properties [1 mark]

2. a 44 to 46 °C. [1 mark]
   b Same as answer to part (a). [1 mark]

3. a As the temperature of a gas decreases, so does its volume [1 mark] also, some of the gases inside will have condensed/changed into liquids. [1 mark]
   b Stay the same. [1 mark]
   c When a gas condenses the atoms or molecules rearrange/get closer together [1 mark] but the number of them stays the same so the mass remains the same /is conserved. [1 mark]

Internal energy and specific latent heat

1. a internal energy [1 mark]
   b Stays the same [1 mark] because temperature does not change during a change of state. [1 mark]

2. 2.26 MJ/kg = 2.26×10⁶ J/kg or 2 260 000 J/kg and 20 g = 0.02 kg [1 mark]; energy transferred = $m L$ = 0.02 × 2.26 × 10⁶ [1 mark] (or 0.02 × 2 260 000) = 45 200 J [1 mark]

3. 10 g = 0.01 kg [1 mark]; energy transferred = $m L$ = 0.01 × 3.34 × 10⁵ [1 mark] = 3340 J [1 mark]

4. $E = m L$, 12 000 = mass × 3.34 × 10⁵ [1 mark]; mass = $\frac{12000}{3.34 \times 10^5}$ [1 mark] = 0.035 928 kg [1 mark] 0.036 kg (2 significant figures) [1 mark]

5. Energy to heat water to boiling point = $m c \Delta\theta$ = 0.25 × 4200 × (100 – 20) [1 mark] = 84 000 J [1 mark]

   Energy to convert water to steam at 100 °C = $m L$ = 0.25 × 2.26 × 10⁶ [1 mark] = 565 000 J [1 mark]

   Total energy required = 84 000 + 565 000 J = 649 000 J [1 mark]

Particle motion in gases

1. a When molecules of gas (in the air) collide with/collide and rebound from the tyre walls [1 mark] they exert forces on the walls. [1 mark]
   b Pressure increases [1 mark] because as the temperature of the gas increases, the air particles move faster [1 mark]; collisions between the particles and the tyre wall occur with more force/there are also more frequent collisions. [1 mark]

2. a The particles move (all the time) [1 mark], the speed of any one particle is random [1 mark], the direction of any one particle is random. [1 mark]
   b Increases [1 mark]

Increasing the pressure of a gas

1. Temperature [1 mark]; mass [1 mark]
2. pV = constant = 120 × 10³ × 5.0 × 10⁻³ [1 mark] = 600 [1 mark]; 75 × 10³ × V_2 = 600 [1 mark]; $V_2 = \frac{600}{75 \times 10^3}$ [1 mark] = 0.008 m³ or 8.0 × 10⁻³ m³ [1 mark]

3. When you push the handle in you are doing work. [1 mark] Doing work on the air inside the pump increases the internal energy of the air/transfers energy to the gas particles in the air [1 mark]; as the internal energy increases the temperature of the gas increases [1 mark]

Section 4: Atomic structure

Protons, neutrons and electrons

1. Around (surrounding/outside) the nucleus [1 mark] at different distances/in specific energy levels/shells. [1 mark]

2. a Protons [1 mark]; neutrons [1 mark]

  b In the nucleus. [1 mark]

3. Electromagnetic radiation is emitted. [1 mark]

4. They absorb electromagnetic radiation. [1 mark]

5. Further from the nucleus. [1 mark]

The size of atoms

1. 1×10^{-10} m [1 mark]

2. a 10 000:1, or 10 000 times bigger [1 mark]

  b Four [1 mark]

  c 1×10^{-14} m [1 mark]

3. 2.70×10^{-10} m [1 mark]

4. a 1.52×10^{-10} m [1 mark]

  b $V = \frac{4}{3} \pi (1.52 \times 10^{-10})^3$ [1 mark] $= 1.47(102) \times 10^{-29}$ m³ [1 mark] 1.5×10^{-29} m³ (2 significant figures) [1 mark]

5. $\frac{1.2 \times 10^{-10}}{1.9 \times 10^{-15}}$ [1 mark] $= 63\,158$ [1 mark] 63 000 to 2 significant figures [1 mark]

Elements and isotopes

1.

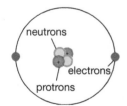

[1 mark for 2 electrons in correct place; 1 mark for 2 neutrons in correct place; 1 mark for 2 protons in correct place]

2. a

Nucleus	Atomic number	Mass number	Number of neutrons
A	88	226	138
B	88	224	136
C	85	226	141
D	86	224	138
E	86	222	136
F	92	226	134

  b A and B [1 mark]; D and E [1 mark]

3. a 84 protons [1 mark]; 126 neutrons [1 mark]

  b $^{218}_{84}$Po [1 mark for 84 in correct place; 1 mark for 218 in correct place]

Electrons and ions

1. a Positive (or +1) [1 mark]

  b 6 protons [1 mark], 8 neutrons [1 mark], 5 electrons [1 mark]

2. 8 protons [1 mark], 8 neutrons [1 mark], 10 electrons [1 mark]

3. 12 protons [1 mark], 12 neutrons [1 mark], 10 electrons [1 mark]

Discovering the structure of the atom

1. a Most passed straight through/not deflected [1 mark], very small proportion were scattered backwards/deflected through large angles. [1 mark]

  b The marks are in three bands according to the level of response.

Level 3 (5/6 marks): A detailed explanation with logical links between clearly identified relevant points. Clearly explains how new evidence led to a change in the model, identifying differences in the models.
Level 2 (3/4 marks): An explanation linking some relevant statements about the evidence. Not all the statements may be linked to explanations.
Level 1 (1/2 marks): Some relevant points are made but with no logical structure.
0: No relevant content

Indicative content:

- Deflection/back scattering of the positively charged alpha particles provided evidence of a very small, central region in atoms where all the positive charge is located.
- When alpha particles passed close by to this region they were repelled by the positive charge.
- That most alpha particles passed straight through was evidence that most of the atom is empty space/mass concentrated in the nucleus.
- The model was changed to include a very small, central, positively charged nucleus.
- The results provided evidence that the plum pudding model was not correct.
- The model of the atom had to change to explain the results.
- Fast travelling alpha particles should not have been bounced back, according to the plum pudding model.
- In the plum pudding model mass is equally distributed throughout the atom.
- In the plum pudding model positive charge is distributed throughout the atom.

2. Replaced old model of electrons surrounding the nucleus anywhere in a cloud [1 mark] with model in which electrons only able to occupy certain energy levels/distances/shells from the nucleus. [1 mark]

Radioactive decay

1. The number of radioactive decays per second. [1 mark]

2. Beta – high speed/fast moving electron from the nucleus. [1 mark] Gamma – electromagnetic radiation. [1 mark]

3. A neutron in the nucleus turns into a proton plus an electron [1 mark]; electron leaves the nucleus. [1 mark]

4. Two neutrons and two protons [1 mark] emitted/ejected from the nucleus. [1 mark]

5. Record count rate and subtract the background count rate. [1 mark]

Comparing alpha, beta and gamma radiation

1.

Radiation type	Approximate range in air	Ionising power (high/medium/low)
alpha	around 5 cm (accept a few cm/1 to 10 cm)	high
beta	around 15 cm (accept tens of centimetres/10 to 90 cm)	medium
gamma	very far/several metres (accept 1–4 m)	low

2. Alpha radiation would not pass through the body/skin (to reach detector) [1 mark]; alpha radiation would damage the body due to high ionising power. [1 mark]

3. The marks are in two bands according to the level of response.

Level 2 (3/4): A detailed and coherent evaluation is provided; comes to a conclusion consistent with the reasoning.
Level 1 (1/2): Some valid, discrete points made. The logic may be unclear and the conclusion, if present, may not be consistent with the reasoning.
0: No relevant content

Indicative content:

- Alpha/beta radiation not very penetrating.
- Gamma source must be used, because alpha and beta radiation would not pass through soil, so unable to be detected.
- Half-life of sodium-24 is long enough for readings to be taken (and find the leak).
- But short enough to minimise harm to living things in the environment.

Radioactive decay equations

1. $^{14}_{6}\text{C} \rightarrow ^{14}_{7}\text{N} + ^{0}_{-1}\text{e}$ [1 mark for each correct missing value]

2. Alpha [1 mark] because mass number decreases by 4 and atomic number decreases by 2. [1 mark]

3. $^{226}_{88}\text{Ra} \rightarrow \, ^{222}_{86}\text{Rn} + \, ^{4}_{2}\text{He}$ [1 mark for each correct component]

4. $^{210}_{84}\text{Po} \rightarrow \, ^{206}_{82}\text{Pb} + \, ^{4}_{2}\text{He}$ [1 mark for each correct component]

Half-lives

1. 1 hour 40 mins = 100 mins = 5 half-lives [1 mark]; $70\,000 \rightarrow 35\,000 \rightarrow 17\,500 \rightarrow 8750 \rightarrow$ $4375 \rightarrow 2187.5$ (Bq) or $\frac{(70\,000)}{2^5} = 2187.5$ [1 mark] 2200 (an average approximate value rounded to whole number as cannot have fractional values for activity.) [1 mark]

2. a Activity halves every 3 days, so after 12 days, 4 half-lives have passed [1 mark]; $280 \rightarrow 140 \rightarrow 70 \rightarrow 35 \rightarrow 17.5$ or $\frac{280}{2^4} = 17.5$ [1 mark] 18 (an average approximate value rounded to whole number as cannot have fractional values for activity) [1 mark]

   b $5.0 \times 10^6 \rightarrow 2\,500\,000 \rightarrow 1\,250\,000 \rightarrow 625\,000$ $\rightarrow 312\,500 \rightarrow 156\,250 \rightarrow 78\,125 \rightarrow 39\,063$. [1 mark] This is 7 half-lives [1 mark]; 7×3 days = 21 days [1 mark]

3. a $128 \rightarrow 64 \rightarrow 32 \rightarrow 16 \rightarrow 8 \rightarrow 4 \rightarrow 2$. [1 mark] This is 6 half-lives [1 mark]; $\frac{24}{6} = 4$ hours [1 mark]

   b 1 half-life = $\frac{1}{2}$; 2 half-lives = $\frac{1}{4}$; 3 half-lives = $\frac{1}{8}$; 4 half-lives = $\frac{1}{16}$; 5 half-lives = $\frac{1}{32}$; therefore 6 half-lives = $\frac{1}{64}$ [1 mark]

4. a Smooth curve through most of the points. [1 mark]

   b Horizontal line at 130 on graph. [1 mark] Vertical line intercepting at 68 ± 1 small square. [1 mark] Half-life: 68 ± 4 s [1 mark] (Allow other construction lines e.g. from 200 and from 100 counts per second)

5. $\frac{375}{6000}$ [1 mark] = $\frac{1}{16}$ [1 mark]

Radioactive contamination

1. Any two of: wear protective clothing (such as lead apron) to absorb radiation; increase distance from the radioactive source; place suitable material between you and the radioactive source (to absorb radiation/ prevent radiation reaching your body). [1 mark each]

2. Alpha particles are more ionising [1 mark], but the activity (of the source) as well as the type of radiation emitted is important [1 mark] (accept dose of radiation in a given time may be higher).

3. Any two of: radioactive material (solid or liquid) comes into contact with their skin, hair or clothing (by touching); breathe in air containing radioactive dust particles or radioactive gas (e.g. radon); swallow food or water containing radioactive dust particles/ radioactive liquid; lick fingers after touching a surface that is radioactively contaminated. [1 mark each]

4. The marks are in two bands according to the level of response:

Level 2 (3/4): A detailed explanation that includes a coherent comparison using correct scientific terminology and including both similarities and differences.
Level 1 (1/2): Some relevant points made. An attempt at comparison may be made, but logic is unclear and unstructured.
0: No relevant content

Indicative content:

- Contamination involves contact with radioactive material/transfer of radioactive material.
- Irradiation involves exposure to radiation from the radioactive source but there is no transfer of radioactive material.
- The irradiated object does not become radioactive itself.
- Once the radioactive source is removed, the object is no longer irradiated/radiation no longer passes through the object so hazard stops.
- Once an object has been radioactively contaminated it is continually exposed to ionising radiation because the source of radioactivity remains with the object.
- Hazard from radioactive contamination is from decay of the contaminating atoms.

Background radiation

1. Any one from: (radioactive) rocks /soil; building materials; cosmic rays (from space); food and drink. [1 mark]

2. a 0.01 Sv [1 mark]

   b Any two of: work at Sellafield; work as a doctor/radiotherapist/dentist/give CT/X-rays scans to patients; work as a flight attendant/pilot; work monitoring the beaches. [1 mark each]

   c The marks are in three bands according to the level of response.

Level 3 (5/6 marks): A detailed and coherent evaluation that considers a range of relevant points about how well the data correlates with the statement, quoting comparisons and comes to a conclusion consistent with the reasoning.
Level 2 (3/4 marks): An attempt is made to relate relevant points within the data and come to a conclusion. The logic may be inconsistent at times but builds towards a coherent argument.
Level 1 (1/2 marks): Discrete relevant points made. The logic may be unclear and the conclusion, if present, may not be consistent with the reasoning.
0: no relevant content
Indicative content: • Radiation dose is a measure of the harm to you. • Medical treatments (X-rays and CT scans) have high doses compared to doses due to eating Cumbrian seafood/ using Cumbrian beaches. • A single CT scan is equivalent to 1000 times the dose from use of beaches. • Doses due to eating Cumbrian seafood/ using Cumbrian beaches are much less than the dose from (average UK) background radiation. • Single CT scan over three times what you receive naturally from average annual natural (background) radiation. • Recreational use of beaches no more harmful than eating a banana. • Recreational use of beaches no more harmful than a single flight to Spain. • People visiting beaches in Cornwall may receive a higher dose due to naturally occurring background radiation.

Uses and hazards of nuclear radiation

1. Destroy/kill/damage healthy body cells. [1 mark]
2. a Gamma rays (are very penetrating and) can be detected outside the body [1 mark]; half-life is short so tracer does not stay radioactive in the body for long (but long enough for readings to be taken/see the results). [1 mark]

   b Any two of: Alpha radiation causes high damage to tumour tissue [1 mark] Half-life is longer so stays radioactive in the body longer giving a higher radiation dose (to kill the tumour) [1 mark]; alpha radiation not very penetrating, so reduces chance of damaging healthy cells around the tumour. [1 mark]

   c Patient's body fluids (faeces, urine, saliva) will be radioactive for several days [1 mark]; using sanitiser does not remove radioactive materials from hands or, washing hands with soap and water will remove radioactive contamination of the skin. [1 mark]

3. As time passes the hazard will decrease [1 mark]; hazard from strontium-90 or caesium-137 will be much reduced/almost zero after about 300 years/ten half-lives [1 mark]; hazard from plutonium-239 will remain for many thousands of years [1 mark]; hazard from uranium will remain for hundreds of millions of years. [1 mark]

Nuclear fission

1. a A uranium-235 nucleus [1 mark] absorbs a neutron [1 mark] (accept neutron hits (uranium) nucleus)

   b Splits into two smaller parts [1 mark]; plus two or three neutrons [1 mark] and emits energy/gamma rays. [1 mark]

2. a Any four of: fission causes 2 or 3 neutrons to be released; each neutron strikes/ absorbed by another (plutonium) nucleus/ atom; making it unstable; each nucleus that absorbs a neutron fissions/splits apart; further neutrons released; that can be absorbed again causing more (plutonium) nuclei to split. [1 mark each]

   b Chain reaction is controlled in a nuclear reactor but uncontrolled in a nuclear bomb. [1 mark]

Nuclear fusion

1. Two small/light nuclei [1 mark], fuse /join to make a larger/heavier nucleus [1 mark], (accept two hydrogen nuclei join to form a helium nucleus for 2 marks)

2. a Tritium has 1 more neutron (in the nucleus). [1 mark]

   b $^4_2$He [1 mark for each correct missing value]

   c Converted into energy (which radiates away) [1 mark]

Section 5: Forces

Scalars and vectors

1. a A scalar quantity only has magnitude. [1 mark] A vector quantity has magnitude and direction. [1 mark]
  b Any suitable example e.g. distance, speed, mass, time, for 1 mark.
  c Any suitable example e.g. displacement, force, velocity, acceleration, momentum, for 1 mark.
2. Distance in the range of 620 m to 660 m. [1 mark] Direction: 072° or 72°E (accept angle in the range of 70° to 74° or accept the angle correctly measured and marked on the diagram. [1 mark]

Speed and velocity

1. $s = vt$, $60\,000 = v \times 240$ [1 mark] $v = \frac{60\,000}{240}$ [1 mark]; 250 m/s [1 mark]; speed $= \frac{250 \times 3600}{1000} =$ 900 km/h [1 mark]
2. 1200 s [1 mark]
3. a C [1 mark]
  b A [1 mark]
  c B [1 mark]
4. a Speed = gradient = $\frac{25-5}{6-2}$ [1 mark] = 5 m/s [1 mark]
  b Evidence that a tangent has been drawn to the curve at 8 s. [1 mark] Speed in the range of 2 m/s to 3 m/s. [1 mark]

Acceleration

1. $\frac{7.8-6.6}{2.0}$ [1 mark] 0.60 m/s² [1 mark]
2. 36 km/h $= \frac{36 \times 1000}{3600} = 10$ m/s and 54 km/h $= \frac{54 \times 1000}{3600} = 15$ m/s. [1 mark] Acceleration $= \frac{15-10}{2.0}$ [1 mark] = 2.5 m/s² [1 mark]
3. $10 = \frac{\text{final velocity} - 10}{2}$. [1 mark] Final velocity = $(2 \times 10) + 10$ [1 mark] 30 m/s [1 mark]
4. a From time = 0 s to time = 10 s [1 mark]
  b From time = 10 s to time = 20 s [1 mark]
  c $\frac{30-10}{20-10}$ [1 mark] = 2 m/s² [1 mark]
  d Either divide area under graph line into segments, e.g. distance = $(10 \times 20) + (\frac{1}{2} \times 10 \times 20)$ [1 mark] = 300 m. [1 mark] Alternatively accept: total number of the squares = 6 [1 mark]; area of each square = 10 × 5 = 50 [1 mark]; distance = 6 × 50 = 300 m [1 mark]

e $300 = v \times 20$ [1 mark]; $v = \frac{300}{20}$ [1 mark] = 15 m/s [1 mark]; $\frac{(15 \times 3600)}{1000} = 54$ km/h [1 mark]
5. Attempt to draw a tangent to the curve at 15 s. [1 mark] Correct data selected from graph for gradient calculation. [1 mark] Acceleration in range 0.85 m/s² to 1.05 m/s² [1 mark]

Equation for uniform acceleration

1. $v^2 - 4^2 = 2 \times 0.25 \times 40$ [1 mark]; $v^2 = 4^2 + (2 \times 0.25 \times 40)$ [1 mark]; 36 gives velocity = $\sqrt{36} = 6.0$ m/s [1 mark]
2. $v^2 - 0 = 2 \times 9.8 \times 50$ [1 mark]; 980 gives velocity $= \sqrt{980} = 31(.304)$ m/s [1 mark] = 31 m/s (2 significant figures) [1 mark]
3. $10^2 - 0 = 2 \times a \times 100$ [1 mark]; Rearranging gives $a = \frac{100}{2 \times 100}$ [1 mark] = 0.50 m/s² [1 mark]

Forces

1. a Give 1 mark for each correctly labelled force arrow.
  b Friction (between tyres and ground) [1 mark]; air resistance [1 mark]; engine driving force/ thrust [1 mark]

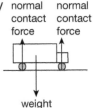

Moment of a force

1. a Moment = $Fd = 1.0 \times (0.50 - 0.30$ [1 mark] = 0.20 N m) [1 mark]
  b (Anticlockwise moment = clockwise moment): $0.20 = X \times (0.85 - 0.50)$ [1 mark]; gives $X = \frac{0.20}{0.35}$ [1 mark] = 0.57(1429) N [1 mark] 0.57 N (2 significant figures) [1 mark]
2. a Moment = $Fd = 1.0 \times (0.50 - 0.30$ [1 mark] = 0.20 N m)
  b (Anticlockwise moment = clockwise moment) $0.20 = 1.5 \times d$ [1 mark]; gives $d = 0.13$ m [1 mark]

Levers and gears

1. a Moment $M = Fd = 1000 \times 0.40$ [1 mark] = 400 N m. [1 mark]
  b $400 = F \times 1.40$ [1 mark] $F = \frac{400}{1.40}$ [1 mark] = 285.7 N [1 mark] 286 N (3 significant figures) [1 mark]
  c $W_{max} \times 0.40 = 300 \times 1.4$ [1 mark]; max weight $W_{max} = \frac{300 \times 1.4}{0.40}$. [1 mark] Gives max weight = 1050 N [1 mark] = 1.05 kN [1 mark]
2. Number of rotations $= \frac{54}{12} = 4.5$ [1 mark]

Pressure in a fluid

1. Pressure $= p = \frac{F}{A} = \frac{5.5}{0.0038}$ [1 mark] $= 1447$
   [1 mark] $= 1.447$ kPa [1 mark] 1.4 kPa
   (2 significant figures) [1 mark]
2. **a** Pressure $p = hpg = 40 \times 1000 \times 9.8$ [1 mark] $=$
   3.92×10^5 Pa [1 mark for standard form] $= 3.9$
   $\times 10^5$ Pa (2 significant figures) [1 mark]
   b Force is normal/90° to the body's surface.
   [1 mark]
   c The pressure increases [1 mark]; there is a greater
   weight of water above the diver. [1 mark]

Atmospheric pressure

1. **a** Air density [1 mark]
   b Pressure $= 44\,000$ Pa [1 mark] (Allow 44 000
   to 46 000 Pa)
   c $45\,000 = \frac{F}{2}$ [1 mark]. Force $= 45\,000 \times 2$
   [1 mark] $= 90\,000$ N [1 mark]
2. The force exert by the atmosphere is due to
   gas molecules colliding with the person's body.
   [1 mark] At altitude the molecules are more spread
   out/have bigger gaps between them. [1 mark] So
   the gas molecules make fewer collisions (in a given
   time) with the person's body [1 mark]

Gravity and weight

1. Weight $= \frac{8.8}{1000} \times 9.8$ [1 mark] $= 0.08624$ N
   [1 mark] 0.086 (2 significant figures) [1 mark]
2. $W = mg$, $4.9 = m \times 9.8$ [1 mark]; mass $= \frac{4.9}{9.8}$
   [1 mark] $= 0.50$ kg [1 mark] $= 500$ g [1 mark]
3. Weight is directly proportional to mass
   [1 mark], so if mass is doubled then weight also
   doubles. [1 mark]

Resultant forces and Newton's first law

1. **a** Resultant force $= 4$ N [1 mark]; to the left.
   [1 mark]
   b Resultant force $= 0$ N [1 mark]
   c The trolley would move with a constant
   velocity (accept speed). [1 mark] According
   to Newton's first law [1 mark], if the resultant
   force on an object/trolley is zero, it continues
   to move with a constant velocity. [1 mark]
2. 1 mark for each correctly
   labelled force in the correct
   direction (regardless of length
   of arrow) (see diagram to right)

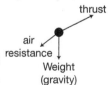

3. **a** Accept force F in the range 24
   to 26 N as measured. [1 mark]

b 1 mark for each correct component arrow
(see diagram below).

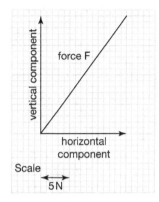

Scale
5 N

c Horizontal component $= 15$ N [1 mark];
vertical component $= 20$ N. [1 mark]

4. **a** See diagram. Vertical
   force (10 N) drawn with
   a suitable scale [1 mark];
   horizontal force (10 N)
   drawn to the same scale
   [1 mark]; resultant force
   drawn in correct direction.
   [1 mark]

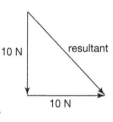

   Size of resultant $= 14$ N [1 mark]

   b Direction shown by any of the angles shown
   in the diagram. [1 mark]

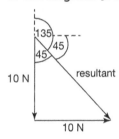

Forces and acceleration

1. Resultant force $= 4800 - 1200 = 3600$ N [1 mark];
   $3600 = 3000 \times a$ [1 mark]; a Acceleration
   $a = \frac{3600}{3000}$ [1 mark] $= 1.2$ m/s² [1 mark]
2. **a** Weight $= mg = 0.42 \times 9.8$ [1 mark] $= 4.116$ N
   [1 mark] 4.1 N (2 significant figures) [1 mark]
   b Resultant force $= 4.1 - 2.1$ [1 mark] $= 2.0$ N
   [1 mark]
   c $2.0 = 0.42 \times a$ [1 mark]; acceleration $= a =$
   $\frac{2.0}{0.42}$ [1 mark] $= 4.7619$ m/s² [1 mark] $=$
   4.8 m/s² (2 significant figures) [1 mark]
3. **a** Acceleration, $a = \dfrac{\text{velocity change}}{\text{time}} = \dfrac{6.2 - 4.2}{4.0}$
   [1 mark] $= 0.50$ m/s² [1 mark]

b Resultant force, $F = ma = 60 \times 0.50$ [1 mark] = 30 N [1 mark]

c Driving force = 30 + 20 [1 mark] = 50 N [1 mark]

4. a The accelerating force is found by multiplying the mass attached (in kg) by gravitational field strength/g/9.8 (N/kg). [1 mark]

b (Left light gate) $0.10 = v \times 0.50$. [1 mark]
Speed = $\frac{0.10}{0.50}$ [1 mark] = 0.20 m/s. [1 mark]
Right light gate: speed = $\frac{0.10}{0.25}$ [1 mark] = 0.40 m/s. [1 mark]

c Equation $v^2 - u^2 = 2as$ selected and data substituted to give $0.4^2 - 0.2^2 = 2 \times a \times 0.5$. [1 mark] Acceleration $a = \frac{0.40^2 - 0.20^2}{2 \times 0.50}$ [1 mark] = 0.12 m/s^2 [1 mark]

d Independent variable: resultant force. [1 mark] Dependent variable: acceleration. [1 mark]

e Graph is a straight line [1 mark] through the origin [1 mark]

Terminal velocity

1. B [1 mark]

2. a Terminal velocity before opening parachute = 50 m/s. [1 mark] Terminal velocity before after opening parachute = 4 m/s. [1 mark]

b Attempt to determine gradient by drawing a tangent to the curve at time = 20 s. [1 mark] Answer in range from 0.6 to 0.75 m/s^2. [1 mark]

c The marks are in three bands according to the level of response.

Level 3 (5/6 marks): Detailed coherent description of the changes in acceleration. A clear explanation with logical links between clearly identified relevant points of reasons for the changes in acceleration.
Level 2 (3/4 marks): Clear description of the changes in acceleration with some correct statements explaining the changes. The logic may be inconsistent at times but builds towards a coherent argument.
Level 1 (1/2 marks): An explanation linking some relevant statements about the changes. Not all the statements may be linked to explanations.
0: No relevant content

Indicative content

- The sky diver's acceleration is greatest as he jumps from the aircraft.
- His acceleration decreases as he falls.
- At 30 s his acceleration becomes zero.
- At the start of his jump his weight is much bigger than air resistance so the resultant downward force is large.
- As he gets faster, the air resistance acting on him gets larger so the resultant force decreases. Therefore the acceleration decreases (but not his speed!).
- At 30 s his weight and air resistance are equal so the resultant force is zero. Therefore the acceleration is zero. He is now travelling at terminal velocity.

Newton's third law

1. a When two objects interact, the forces they exert on each other are equal and opposite. [1 mark]

b Normal contact force [1 mark] exerted by (the top of) the table (on the book). [1 mark]

c Weight/force of gravity [1 mark] exerted by the Earth (on the book). [1 mark]

d Normal contact force [1 mark] exerted by the book [1 mark] on (the top of) the table. [1 mark]

e Force of gravity [1 mark] exerted by the book [1 mark] on the Earth. [1 mark]

Work done and energy transfer

1. a Change of 0.60 kN to 600 N [1 mark]; work done = $Fs = 600 \times 20$ [1 mark] = 12 000 J [1 mark]
Useful output power = $\frac{\text{work done}}{\text{time}} = \frac{12\,000}{20}$ [1 mark] = 600 W [1 mark]

b Increase in gravitational potential energy = $mgh = 200 \times 9.8 \times 5$ [1 mark] = 9800 J [1 mark]

c Energy transferred to (thermal energy store of) surroundings /energy dissipated (or 'wasted') due to friction. [1 mark]

2. a Force = $mg = (600 + 400) \times 9.8$ [1 mark] = 9800 N [1 mark]

b Work done = $Fs = 9800 \times 10$ [1 mark] = 98 000 J [1 mark]
Useful output power = $\frac{98\,000}{10}$ [1 mark] = 9800 W [1 mark]

3. a Work done = $Fs = 5000 \times 1000$ [1 mark] = 5 000 000 J. [1 mark]

b Time = distance/speed = $\frac{1000}{100}$ = 10 s [1 mark]

c Useful output power = $\frac{\text{work done}}{\text{time}} = \frac{5\,000\,000}{10}$ [1 mark] = 500 000 W [1 mark]

Answers

Stopping distance

1. **a** Distance travelled during the driver's reaction time. [1 mark] 1 mark for any one of the following examples: tiredness, alcohol, drugs, being distracted (e.g. mobile phone).

   b Distance travelled while a braking force is being applied. [1 mark] 1 mark for any one of the following examples: wet conditions, diesel spillage, icy conditions, worn tyres, worn brakes, gradient.

   c Stopping distance = 26 m (accept in range 25 to 27 m). [1 mark]

   d Stopping distance = 90 m (accept in range 89 to 91 m). [1 mark]

   e The student's prediction is incorrect. [1 mark] Suitable reason given referring to the data e.g. Doubling the speed (from 15 to 30 m/s) does not double the stopping distance, or doubling the speed more than trebles the stopping distance [1 mark]

2. **a** Reaction time = $\frac{distance}{speed} = \frac{14}{20}$ [1 mark] = 0.7 s [1 mark]

   b Work done = original kinetic energy = $\frac{1}{2} \times 1000 \times 20^2$ [1 mark] = 200 000 J. [1 mark] Work done = 200 000 = braking force × 40 [1 mark]; braking force = $\frac{200\,000}{40}$ [1 mark] = 5000 N [1 mark] Allow credit for correct calculation using $v^2 - u^2 = 2as$

   c Car's store of kinetic energy decreases [1 mark]; store of thermal energy (in the surrounding air/brakes and tyres/road) increases [1 mark]; brakes get very hot/may over-heat. [1 mark]

Force and extension

1. **a** The weight attached to the spring exerts a downward force. [1 mark] The normal contact force exerted by the clamp exerts an upward force on the spring. [1 mark]

   b Extension = 9.5 − 4.5 = 5.0 cm = 0.050 m [1 mark]; 2.0 = $k \times 0.05$ [1 mark]; spring constant $k = \frac{2.0}{0.05}$ [1 mark] = 40 N/m. [1 mark]

   c Elastic potential energy = $\frac{1}{2} ke^2 = \frac{1}{2} \times 40 \times 0.050^2$ [1 mark] = 0.050 J [1 mark]

2. **a** The marks are in two bands according to the level of response.

   > Level 2 (3/4 marks): Clear plan with all steps presented in a logical sequence including reference to minimising errors.

   > Level 1 (1/2 marks): Simple statements are made about some of the relevant parts of the method but the steps may not be in an order that makes sense and may not lead to the production of valid results.

   > 0: No relevant content

   Indicative content:
   - Make sure metre rule is clamped vertically/parallel to the spring.
   - Use pointer to make sure that you measure the spring length from the same point on the spring each time.
   - Measure unstretched length of spring.
   - Add a (known) weight to the spring and measure the length.
   - Make sure that the spring is not oscillating (bouncing or swinging) when you measure its length.
   - Calculate extension by subtracting unstretched length from stretched length.
   - Add additional weights and repeat the measurements to produce a set of force and extension data.
   - Repeat procedure and calculate average extension for each weight attached.

   b 1 mark for each correctly plotted point. [3 marks]

   c Suitable best fit line. [1 mark]

   d Extension is directly proportional to force [1 mark] since graph is a straight line through origin [1 mark]

   e Gradient in the range 2.9 to 3.1 cm/N [1 mark] answer given to 2 significant figures. [1 mark]

   f Answer in the range 0.32 to 0.34 N/cm [1 mark] answer given to 2 significant figures. [1 mark]

Momentum

1. **a** Vector [1 mark]

   b 36 km/h = $\frac{36 \times 1000}{3600}$ = 10 m/s [1 mark]; momentum = $mv = 850 \times 10$ [1 mark] = 8500 kg m/s [1 mark]

2. Momentum change = $(800 \times 15) - (800 \times 5)$ [1 mark] = 8000 kg m/s [1 mark]

3. Momentum = $2.4 \times 10^{-21} = 1.7 \times 10^{-27} \times v$. [1 mark] Velocity $v = \frac{2.4 \times 10^{-21}}{1.7 \times 10^{-27}}$ [1 mark] = 1.411765×10^6 m/s [1 mark] = 1.4×10^6 m/s (2 significant figures) [1 mark]

Conservation of momentum

1. a Momentum = mv = 0.17 × 5.0 [1 mark] = 0.85 kg m/s. [1 mark]

  b Momentum after the collision = momentum before the collision [1 mark]; (0.17 × v) + (0.16 × 4.0) = 0.85 [1 mark]
Velocity $v = \frac{0.85 - 0.64}{0.17}$ [1 mark] = 1.23529 m/s [1 mark] 1.2 m/s (2 significant figures) [1 mark]

2. a Momentum before collision = (1000 × 8.0) + (800 × 5.0) [1 mark] = 12 000 kg m/s. [1 mark]

  b Momentum after the collision = momentum before the collision [1 mark]; (1000 + 800) × v = 12 000 [1 mark] Velocity = $v = \frac{12000}{1800}$ [1 mark] = 6.6667 m/s [1 mark] 6.7 m/s (2 significant figures) [1 mark]

Rate of change of momentum

1. a Momentum = mv = 50 × 5.0 [1 mark] = 250 kg m/s [1 mark]

  b Force = $\frac{\text{change in momentum}}{\text{time}} = \frac{250}{0.50}$ [1 mark] = 500 N [1 mark]

  c Same momentum change. [1 mark] Impact force would be greater [1 mark] because the impact time is smaller. [1 mark]

2. a Car A: rate of change of momentum = $\frac{\text{change in momentum}}{\text{time}} = \frac{1000 \times 6.0}{0.10}$ [1 mark] = 60 000 kg m/s² [1 mark]
Car B: rate of change of momentum = $\frac{\text{change in momentum}}{\text{time}} = \frac{800 \times 8.0}{0.10}$ [1 mark] = 64 000 kg m/s² [1 mark]

  b Car B experiences the greatest impact force [1 mark] because it has the greatest rate of change of momentum [1 mark]

Section 6: Waves

Transverse and longitudinal waves

1. In the same direction as the wave. [1 mark]

2. Seismic S waves and microwaves. [1 mark]

3. A compression is where the (gas) particles are closest together/region of high(er) pressure. [1 mark] A rarefaction is where the (gas) particles are furthest apart/ region of low(er) pressure. [1 mark]

4. If the sound wave moved air away from the string this would create a vacuum (around the string). [1 mark]

Frequency and period

1. Period = $\frac{1}{440}$ [1 mark] = 0.002273 (s) [1 mark] = 2.273 ms [1 mark] 2.3 ms (2 significant figures) [1 mark]

2. 0.4 = $\frac{1}{f}$ [1 mark]; $f = \frac{1}{0.4}$ [1 mark] = 2.5 (Hz) [1 mark]

3. Period = $\frac{1}{15}$ [1 mark] = 0.066667 s [1 mark] 0.067 s (2 significant figures) [1 mark]

4. Period = $\frac{1}{20}$ [1 mark] = 0.05 s [1 mark]

Wave calculations

1. 909 kHz = 909 000 Hz [1 mark]; 3.0 × 10⁸ = 909 000 × λ [1 mark]; λ = $\frac{3 \times 10^8}{909\,000}$ [1 mark] = 330 (m) [1 mark]

2. a Measure the distance between as many ripples as possible (any practical number stated) and divide total length by the number of ripples (minus 1 because the number of wavelengths is one less than the number of ripples). [1 mark]

  b Time how long it takes the wave to travel between two points/the length of the ripple tank [1 mark], use distance/time to calculate speed. [1 mark]

  c Random errors when stopping and starting the stopwatch. [1 mark]

  d $\frac{(0.232 + 0.250 + 0.241)}{3}$ = 0.241 (m/s) [1 mark]

  e Amount of uncertainty = $\frac{(0.25 - 0.232)}{2}$ [1 mark] = ±0.009 (m/s) [1 mark] (ignore missing ±)

3. Wavelength is longer in metal (wavelength shorter in air) [1 mark], (because) wavelength is wave velocity divided by frequency and frequency does not change. [1 mark] Allow wavelength and wave speed are directly proportional [1 mark]

4. (Minimum (shortest) period will be for the highest frequency) wavelength of the highest frequency visible light is 400 nm [1 mark]; 400 nm is 4 × 10⁻⁷ m or 0.000 000 4 m [1 mark]; highest frequency = $\frac{3 \times 10^8}{4 \times 10^{-7}}$ [1 mark]; minimum period = $\frac{1}{f} = \frac{4 \times 10^{-7}}{3 \times 10^8}$ [1 mark] = 1.33 × 10⁻¹⁵ s [1 mark] 1 × 10⁻¹⁵ s (1 significant figure) [1 mark]

Reflection and refraction of waves

1. Reflection [1 mark]

2. Some of the light is reflected [1 mark], some is absorbed. [1 mark]

3. Light rays from one direction [1 mark] are reflected (scattered) in all directions. [1 mark] Diffuse reflection [1 mark] if no other marks awarded.

4. **a** Angle marked between the incident ray and the normal line, and labelled 'angle of incidence'. [1 mark]

   b Draw the path of the ray that leaves the block. [1 mark] Remove the block and join the points where the ray entered and left the block. [1 mark] Use a protractor to measure the angle between the transmitted ray (in the block) and the normal (for the incident ray). [1 mark]

   c Differences for the two materials are small (one or two degrees) [1 mark]; difference could be due to measurement uncertainty. [1 mark]

   d Repeat measurement of each angle [1 mark]; test more than four angles (over a wide range). [1 mark]

5. Light has a different velocity in air and in water. [1 mark]

Sound waves

1. 20 Hz to 20 kHz [1 mark]
2. Vibrates/sound waves in air are converted to vibrations of the solid eardrum. [1 mark]
3. Vibrating drum causes alternating compressions/rarefactions of the air (pressure variations in the air) [1 mark]; sound wave (in air) produced. [1 mark]
4. **a** Time for 1 echo to return is too short to measure accurately (due to random errors/human reaction time)/large timing error compared to time for 1 echo. [1 mark]

   b Clap at the exact moment you hear the echo (and repeat) [1 mark]; time how long it takes to takes to hear a large number of echoes and divide by number of echoes [1 mark]; reduces effect of random timing errors. [1 mark]

5. Higher or lower frequency sound waves (entering the ear) do not produce vibrations (of parts of the inner ear) [1 mark], so no sound is heard for those frequencies. [1 mark]

Ultrasound and echo sounding

1. Ultrasound has a higher frequency. [1 mark]
2. Any three of: some of the ultrasound is reflected; some is transmitted; some is absorbed; changes speed/velocity; change in direction of travel. [1 mark each]
3. **a** 240 ms = 0.24 s [1 mark]; distance travelled = 1500×0.24 [1 mark] = 360 m [1 mark]

   b depth = 360 m/2 = 180 m [1 mark]
4. Time of echo is 4×20 μs = 80 μs [1 mark]; 80 μs = 0.00008 s or 8×10^{-5} s [1 mark];

distance travelled = 6000×0.00008 [1 mark] = 0.48 m [1 mark]; depth = 0.48 m/2 = 0.24 m [1 mark]

5. Ultrasound is (partially) reflected from boundary between different tissues [1 mark], remainder passes through (transmitted) and may be reflected by a deeper boundary [1 mark]; ultrasound travels at different speeds in different tissues [1 mark], echoes arriving at different times at the detector are interpreted as images. [1 mark]

6. The marks are in two bands according to the level of response:

Level 2 (3/4): A detailed explanation is provided that includes a coherent comparison using scientific terms correctly and including both similarities and differences.
Level 1 (1/2): Some relevant points made. An attempt at comparison may be made, but logic is unclear and unstructured.
0: No relevant content

Indicative content:

Similarities:

- both are waves and can be reflected/refracted/transmitted/absorbed.

Differences:

- ultrasound is a longitudinal wave, ultraviolet is a transverse wave
- in ultrasound waves, particles oscillate parallel to the direction of wave travel
- in ultraviolet waves the oscillations/vibrations are at right angles to the direction of wave travel
- ultrasound needs a medium to travel/cannot travel through a vacuum
- ultraviolet can travel through a vacuum
- ultraviolet is an electromagnetic wave
- ultraviolet has a higher frequency than ultrasound
- ultrasound has a lower speed than ultraviolet: speed in air around 330 m/s
- ultraviolet travels at same speed as light, 3×10^8 m/s
- ultraviolet is ionising radiation and can cause harm to humans/increase risk of skin cancer
- ultrasound is not ionising radiation/does not cause harm.

Seismic waves

1. S-waves can travel through solids but not through liquids. [1 mark]

Answers

2. P-waves are longitudinal and S-waves are transverse. [1 mark] P-waves can travel through liquids but S-waves cannot. [1 mark]

3. **a** Travel at different speeds in different rocks/layers [1 mark], which causes refraction (at the boundary). [1 mark]

   b Part of the Earth's core is liquid. [1 mark]

The electromagnetic spectrum

1. Radio waves have longer wavelength [1 mark] and lower frequency. [1 mark]

2. Infrared waves have longer wavelength [1 mark] and lower frequency. [1 mark]

3. The material that absorbs the electromagnetic wave/radiation. [1 mark]

4. Red light, 400 nm. [1 mark]

5. The marks are in two bands according to the level of response:

Level 2 (3/4): A detailed explanation is provided that includes a coherent comparison using correct scientific terminology and including both similarities and differences.
Level 1 (1/2): Some relevant points made. An attempt at comparison may be made, but logic is unclear and unstructured.
0: No relevant content

Indicative content:

Similarities:
- both electromagnetic, transverse waves
- both travel at the same speed in a vacuum
- both travel through a vacuum and transfer energy
- both have extremely short wavelengths compared to other electromagnetic radiation
- both very penetrating/pass through skin and soft tissue/not absorbed
- both can be reflected, transmitted or absorbed
- both are ionising radiation which is harmful/mutate genes/cause cancer
- both used in hospitals to create images of the inside of the human body
- both can be used to destroy tumours.

Differences:
- X-rays have longer wavelength and shorter frequency
- gamma rays are produced by changes in the nucleus of an atom/emitted by the nucleus of radioactive atoms
- X-rays are absorbed by bone but gamma (mostly) pass through bone
- difference in absorption of X-rays by different materials in body mean X-rays are used to produce photographs of bones
- medical images produced using gamma rays rely on gamma rays passing through *all* the body.

Refraction and wavefronts

1. Change in velocity. [1 mark]

2. **a** Change direction, but stay parallel to each other. [1 mark]

   b

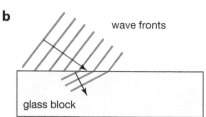

   Refracted wave fronts all straight lines, parallel and joined to the wave fronts in air [1 mark]; changed direction and closer together. [1 mark]

   c Any two of: the part of the wave front that enters the glass first is slowed down; the part that is still in air is travelling faster; one side of the wave front will slow down before the other side. [1 mark each]

Emission and absorption of infrared radiation

1. All objects both emit and absorb infrared radiation, whether they are hot or cool. [1 mark]

2. **a** Independent: colour/nature of surface [1 mark]; Dependent: time to reach 15 °C. [1 mark]

   b Any two of: mass of water, area/shape of can, position in the room, lid/no lid. [1 mark each]

3. **a** 300 nm to about 2750 nm (accept to nearest 100). [1 mark]

   b 10 to 380 nm [1 mark] 2700 to 4000 nm (accept to nearest 100). [1 mark]

   c Any two of: some infrared wavelengths are not transmitted as well as others; some (infrared) wavelengths in the range 700 to 1800 nm are slightly absorbed; for wavelengths longer than about 2750 nm infrared absorption is high (answer must refer to relevant data from graph to gain full marks). [1 mark each]

d All the wavelengths of visible light are transmitted (more or less) equally [1 mark]; no wavelengths (colours) are absorbed or reflected/wavelengths (colours) are absorbed and reflected more or less equally. [1 mark]

4. a Hold detector at same distance from each side, hold the sensor at right angles to the middle of the face each time. [1 mark]

b So that the surfaces reach an even temperature/surfaces heat up to the temperature of the water. [1 mark]

c The other variable (nature of surface) is not continuous/is categoric. [1 mark]

Uses and hazards of the electromagnetic spectrum

1. Microwave [1 mark]; infrared. [1 mark]

2. *Either* increased risk of skin cancer *or* causes skin to age prematurely. [1 mark]

3. a Most food has a high water content [1 mark], so absorbs the energy transferred by the microwaves. [1 mark]

b Glass and plastic allow microwaves to pass through them. [1 mark]

4. Glass absorbs ultraviolet [1 mark], but transmits (some/most of) visible light. [1 mark]

5. a Infrared. [1 mark]

b The person emits (gives out) infrared radiation. [1 mark]

c Black/opaque materials absorb all colours (wavelengths) of visible light *or* block all colours (wavelengths) visible light [1 mark]; but transmit infrared (are transparent to infrared)/do not absorb infrared. [1 mark]

Radio waves

1. Oscillating/changing current (in electric circuit). [1 mark]

2. Alternating current is produced in the electrical circuit [1 mark] with a frequency that matches that of the radio waves. [1 mark]

3. Atmosphere does not absorb the energy transferred by the radio waves [1 mark], so radio waves pass through/are transmitted (to reach homes/TVs). [1 mark]

Colour

1. a 3.9×10^{-7} m [1 mark]

b 7.7×10^{14} Hz [1 mark]

2. All colours (wavelengths) are absorbed except green [1 mark]; only green light is transmitted. [1 mark]

3. a Red light reflected (by the flower) [1 mark]; all other colours (wavelengths) are absorbed. [1 mark]

b Black [1 mark] because red flower only reflects red light and only blue light is incident on it. [1 mark]

Lenses

1. ↕

2. Converges rays [1 mark] to a focus/to form an image. [1 mark]

3. The marks are in two bands according to the level of response:

Level 2 (3/4): The method is described clearly, with steps presented in a logical sequence that would produce valid data.
Level 1 (1/2): Simple statements are made about some of the relevant parts of the method but the steps may not be in an order that makes sense.
0: No relevant content

Indicative content:

- Hold lens in front of a screen (or flat, white wall).
- Choose an object that is a long way away (so that rays from the object are nearly parallel).
- Project the image of the object onto a screen.
- Move the lens (or the screen) until the image is sharp (in focus).
- Measure the distance between the (centre of) the lens and the image.

4. a No ruler, penalise 1 mark; ray that continues from the top of the object through centre of lens [1 mark]; horizontal ray from the top of the object, refracted by the lens and continued through F on the right-hand side [1 mark]; back projections of these rays (shown as dotted lines) [1 mark]; upright arrow drawn where rays cross, 30 mm to left of lens. [1 mark]

b Magnification = 3 cm / 2 cm [1 mark] = 1.5 [1 mark]

c Virtual [1 mark]

5. a No ruler, penalise 1 mark; ray that continues from the top of the object through centre of lens [1 mark]; horizontal ray from the top of the object, refracted by the lens and continued through F on the right-hand side [1 mark]; inverted arrow drawn where rays cross, 30 mm to right of lens. [1 mark]

153

b Magnification = 1.5 cm / 3 cm [1 mark] = 0.5 [1 mark] (accept values for image height ±1 mm).

c Real [1 mark]

A perfect black body

1. No, because it transmits gamma rays/a black body does not transmit any radiation/a black body absorbs all radiation. [1 mark]
2. A perfect black body. [1 mark]
3. Radiation emitted at all wavelengths/ continuous spectrum. [1 mark]
4. Wavelength at which most energy emitted per second (peak intensity) occurs decreases. [1 mark] (Accept converse: peak intensity occurs at greater frequencies.)
5. It is also emitting infrared radiation [1 mark]; if it emits and absorbs energy at same rate/does not gain more energy than it loses [1 mark]; will remain at same temperature. [1 mark]

Temperature of the Earth

1.

Rate at which object absorbs radiation	Temperature of the object
greater than the rate of emission	increases
equal to the rate of emission	remains the same
less than the rate of emission	decreases

2. **a** Increase [1 mark]

b Any reasonable suggestion such as colour/ texture of surface, amount of shiny cover (such as ice), amount of dark surface. [1 mark]

c Increase of gases in the atmosphere (such as water vapour and carbon dioxide) that absorb electromagnetic radiation/amount of cloud cover that reflects radiation. [1 mark]

Section 7: Magnetism and electromagnetism

Magnets and magnetic forces

1. The force is repulsive. [1 mark] The force is a non-contact force. [1 mark]

2. The marks are in two bands according to the level of response.

Level 2 (3/4 marks): A detailed coherent explanation using appropriate terminology. Points are made in a logical sequence.
Level 1 (1/2 marks): Some relevant content but may lack detail or relevance of facts may not be clear.
0: No relevant content

Indicative contact:

- The magnetic field of the permanent magnet induces (temporary) magnetism in the nails.
- The iron nails which were unmagnetised are now magnetised /each nail becomes an induced magnet.
- The head of the top nail/induced magnet is attracted to the (permanent) magnet.
- The point of one nail is attracted to the head of the next nail.
- When the top nail is moved away from the magnet, the nails stop being induced magnets.
- When the nails stop being induced magnets, they stop exerting forces on each other.

Magnetic fields

1. Copper [1 mark]; aluminium. [1 mark]
2. **a** The direction of the force exerted on a north pole [1 mark] placed at the point. [1 mark] Alternatively, give 1 mark for: from a north pole to a south pole.

b Arrows correct on both A and C [1 mark] (see diagram below). Arrows correct on both B and D [1 mark] (see diagram below).

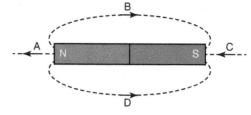

3. The magnet aligns with the Earth's magnetic field. [1 mark] The north pole of the magnet points North/towards the North Pole of the Earth. [1 mark]

The magnetic effect of an electric current

1. **a** Three concentric circles drawn [1 mark] getting further apart. [1 mark] One or more

arrows indicating an anticlockwise direction (arrows must be in **same** direction). [1 mark]

b Wire shaped to form a solenoid/coil. [1 mark] Iron core placed inside the coil. [1 mark]

2. The marks are in three bands according to the level of response.

Level 3 (5/6 marks): A detailed and coherent explanation describing all steps in the correct sequence.
Level 2 (3/4 marks): The majority of steps are described clearly and in the correct sequence.
Level 1 (1/2 marks): Some relevant statements but lacks detail and the steps are not logically linked.
0: No relevant content

Indicative content:

- The current in the coil of wire wrapped around the electromagnet magnetises the electromagnet.
- The magnetic field of the electromagnet attracts the iron armature/strip.
- The hammer hits the gong.
- The contact (at C) is broken when the strip moves away from the contact screw.
- Current stops.
- The electromagnet stops being magnetic.
- The springy metal strip pulls the iron armature back.

- The contact (at C) is made again (circuit complete again).
- Current passes again.
- The process repeats (so hammer keeps hitting the gong, so long as the switch is held down).

Fleming's left-hand rule

1. Vertically downwards. [1 mark]

2. **a** (Vertically) upwards. [1 mark]

   b 200 mT = 0.20 T and 5.0 cm to 0.050 m [1 mark]; magnetic force $F = BIL = 0.20 \times 1.0 \times 0.050$ [1 mark] = 0.010 N. [1 mark]

   c *Either*: Add another cell to the battery/increase the potential difference of the power supply [1 mark] to increase the current. [1 mark] *Or*: replace the magnets with stronger magnets/double up the magnets [1 mark] to increase the magnetic flux density. [1 mark] *Or*: replace the magnets with longer magnets [1 mark]

to increase the length of the magnetic interaction [1 mark]

d *Either*: Switch the wire's connections to the battery [1 mark] to reverse the direction of the current in the wire. [1 mark] *Or*: Swap the magnets round [1 mark] to reverse the direction of the magnetic field. [1 mark]

Electric motors

1. The marks are in three bands according to the level of response.

Level 3 (5/6 marks): A coherent, detailed explanation. The points are made in a logical sequence with logical links between relevant points made.
Level 2 (3/4 marks): A coherent description is provided but may lack some detail and logical structure.
Level 1 (1/2 marks): A few relevant points but lacks detail and logical structure.
0: No relevant content

Indicative content:

- The coil is made up of a wire carrying an electric current in a magnetic field.
- The magnets (producing the field) and the coil exert a (magnetic) force on each other.
- The current in opposite sides of the coil is in opposite directions.
- So the forces on the sides of the coil are in opposite directions
- The force on the side of the coil nearest the north pole is upwards.
- The force on the side of the coil nearest the south pole is downwards.
- The (pair of) forces create a moment/turning effect.
- The moment/turning effect acts around the coil's axis causing the coil to start to rotate
- The momentum of the coil carries it through the vertical position.
- The sides of the coil have now swapped positions.
- But the halves of the split ring have changed contact from one brush to the other reversing the current direction (in the coil).
- So the side of the coil nearest the north pole still experiences an upward force, and the other side a downward force.
- The coil continues to rotate in the same direction.

Loudspeakers

1. a Right [1 mark]

 b Right [1 mark]

 c The marks are in two bands according to the level of response.

> Level 2 (3/4 marks): A detailed coherent explanation with points made in a logical sequence.
>
> Level 1 (1/2 marks): Some relevant points but lacking in detail and in no logical sequence.
>
> 0: No relevant content
>
> **Indicative content:**
> - When the current in the coil is in one direction, the coil/cone is forced to the right.
> - When the current reverses the coil/cone is forced to the left.
> - When the coil is connected to an alternating potential difference, the direction of the current keeps reversing
> - So the coil/cone repeatedly moves left and right (vibrates).
> - If the coil is connected to a battery current flows in one direction in the coil.
> - The force on the coil (and cone) is always in the same direction (so the cone does not vibrate).

Induced potential

1. a Relative movement between a conductor/wire/coil and a magnetic field [1 mark] induces a potential difference across the ends of the conductor. [1 mark]

 b The conductor/wire/coil must be part of a complete circuit. [1 mark]

2. a The marks are in three bands according to the level of response.

> Level 3 (5/6 marks): Detailed, coherent descriptions and explanations using correct terminology. A logical link is made between each observation and its corresponding explanation.
>
> Level 2 (3/4 marks): The observed effects are described with suitable explanations being provided but may lack detail and logical links.

> Level 1 (1/2 marks): Some relevant content
>
> 0: No relevant content
>
> **Indicative content:**
> - When the magnet is moved into the coil, a (non-zero) reading is registered on the voltmeter.
> - Moving the magnet into the coil increases the strength of the (magnetic) field near the coil. Changing the strength of the magnetic field near the copper coil induces a potential difference across the ends of the coil.
> - If the magnet is held stationary inside the coil, the voltmeter reads zero.
> - If the magnet is held stationary inside the coil, there is no change in the magnetic field near the coil so there is no induced potential.
> - If the magnet is moved out of the coil, there is an opposite non-zero reading on the voltmeter.
> - Moving the magnet out of the coil decreases the strength of the (magnetic) field near the coil.
> - Changing the strength of the magnetic field near the copper coil, induces a potential difference across the ends of the coil.
> - The induced potential difference is either positive or negative depending on whether the magnet is moved into or out of the coil.

 b −20 mA. [1 mark]

 c The (induced) current/magnetic field tries to stop the magnet being moved into the coil/opposes movement. [1 mark]

 d The (induced) current/magnetic field tries to stop the magnet being moved out of the coil/opposes movement. [1 mark]

Uses of the generator effect

1. a p.d. = 2 V [1 mark]

 b Time = 0.4 s [1 mark]

 c Number of rotations = 2.5 [1 mark]

 d Max output p.d. increases [1 mark]; time for 1 complete rotation decreases. [1 mark]

2. Correct graph is shown below. Correct shape with no negative peaks. [1 mark] Max p.d. = 5 V. [1 mark] Time between peaks is 0.05 s. [1 mark]

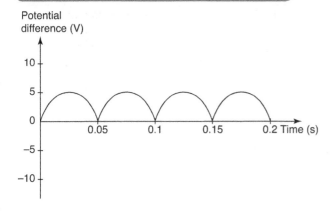

Microphones

1. a The diaphragm is attached to the coil so the coil also vibrates. [1 mark] The coil is moving relative to a magnetic field [1 mark] inducing an alternating potential difference. [1 mark]

b The generator effect [1 mark]

c Alternating [1 mark]

Transformers

1. 95 [1 mark]

2. a Step-down [1 mark]

b Iron is magnetically soft [1 mark] so is easily magnetised and demagnetised [1 mark]

c $\frac{230}{12} = \frac{500}{n_s}$. [1 mark] Rearranging gives $n_s = \frac{500 \times 12}{230}$ or $\frac{12}{230} = \frac{n_s}{500}$ [1 mark] = 26.09 [1 mark] = 26 (2 significant figures) [1 mark]

d $12 \times I_s = 230 \times 0.40$ [1 mark]; $I_s = \frac{230 \times 0.40}{12}$ [1 mark] 7.667 A [1 mark] 7.7 A (2 significant figures) [1 mark]

e A p.d. is induced in the secondary coil if the magnetic field inside the iron core is changing. [1 mark] The primary coil must carry an alternating current to create a changing magnetic field (in the iron core). [1 mark] The current from a battery is constant (so wouldn't produce a changing magnetic field). [1 mark]

3. a $24 = 12 \times I$ [1 mark]; $I = \frac{24}{12}$ [1 mark] = 2.0 A [1 mark]

b $12 \times 2.0 = 230 \times I_p$ [1 mark]; $I_p = \frac{12 \times 2.0}{230}$ [1 mark] = 0.104 A [1 mark] 0.10 A (2 significant figures) [1 mark]

c Some power/energy is dissipated as heat [1 mark] by the current flowing in the coils (in the transformer). [1 mark] *Or* the transformer is less than 100% efficient [1 mark] and so some energy is dissipated as heat [1 mark]

Our Solar System

1. Planets orbit the Sun. [1 mark] Moons orbit planets. [1 mark]

2. a 100 [1 mark] (accept 10^2)

b 2. [1 mark]

3. a Formed from dust/gas/nebula [1 mark] pulled together by gravity/force of gravity/gravitational attraction. [1 mark]

b Nuclear fusion (accept fusion) [1 mark] of (small/hydrogen) nuclei [1 mark] produces more massive (helium) nuclei [1 mark] releasing energy in the process. [1 mark]

The life cycle of a star

1. a 1 mark each for red giant and white dwarf (see diagram below).

b 1 mark each for supernova and neutron star (see diagram below).

2. The marks are in two bands according to the level of response.

Level 2 (3/4 marks): A coherent description covering all major points using the correct scientific terminology is provided. The points are made in a logical sequence.
Level 1 (1/2 marks): Some relevant content but may lack detail. Points may not follow a logical sequence.
No relevant content: 0

Indicative content:

- When a high mass star has used up its nuclear fuel/stops (nuclear) fusion, it collapses and explodes.
- The explosion is called a supernova.
- During the supernova, the high temperature causes the fusion of nuclei larger than iron.
- Explosion also blows the outer layers of the star into space
- The power of the explosion drives these heavy atoms throughout the galaxy.

Orbital motion, natural and artificial satellites

1. **a** Smooth curve through points. [1 mark]
   b As distance increases speed decreases. [1 mark]
   c Accept in the range 4 to 6 km/s. [1 mark]
   d A planet orbits a star/Sun [1 mark] whereas a moon orbits a planet. [1 mark]
   e Time of orbit $= 27 \times 24 \times 60 \times 60$ [1 mark]; $2.4 \times 10^6 = v \times (27 \times 24 \times 60 \times 60)$. [1 mark] Rearranging gives speed $v = \frac{2.4 \times 10^6}{27 \times 24 \times 60 \times 60}$
   [1 mark] $= 1.029$ km/s [1 mark] 1.0 km/s (2 significant figures). [1 mark]

2. **a** The satellite will fall towards Earth/lose height. [1 mark]
   b The satellite will move further away (from Earth) into space. [1 mark]
   c Number of orbits $= \frac{24 \times 60}{100}$ [1 mark] $= 14.4$ [1 mark] 14 (rounded) [1 mark]
   d 1 mark for any one of the following (nearer) so The satellite's instruments are able to make more detailed images/measurements. The satellite passes over the Earth many times in one day so can make frequent measurements. The satellite passes over the Earth many times in one day so is more likely to be able to detect changes.

Red-shift

1. **a** The shift in wavelength towards the red end of the spectrum (accept: the increase in wavelength) [1 mark] of the light (arriving at Earth) from an object/galaxy [1 mark] moving away (from an observer). [1 mark]
   b The speed/velocity (of the galaxy). [1 mark]

2. **a** (Recession) speed is *directly* proportional to distance [1 mark], because the graph is a straight line through the origin. [1 mark]

b The marks are in two bands according to the level of response.

Level 2 (3/4 marks): A coherent detailed description of the Big Bang theory and how it is supported by the graph.

Level 1 (1/2 marks): Some relevant content but may lack detail.

0: No relevant content

Indicative content:

- The Big Bang theory suggests that the universe began in a very small region.
- (The small region) was (very) hot and dense.
- A rapid expansion/explosion occurred (sending matter outwards).
- Galaxies have been moving away from one another ever since
- The universe is expanding/space (between the galaxies) is expanding
- The graph provides evidence that that the further away any galaxy is, the faster it is moving away.
- This is evidence that the universe is expanding.
- The expansion shown by the graph suggest the universe started at a single point (of origin)

c Either, scientific theories have to be extensively scrutinised/tested or, can only have confidence in a scientific theory if it is supported by a lot of evidence. [1 mark] (Ignore 'proves Big Bang theory'.)

Dark matter and dark energy

1. Number of stars $= \frac{1 \times 10^{42}}{5 \times 10^{30}}$ [1 mark] $= 2 \times 10^{11}$
   [1 mark] $= 200$ billion [1 mark]

2. **a** At short distances (close to the centre of the galaxy) curves X and Y follow the same trend/have the same shape. [1 mark] As the distance increases, curve X shows a slight reduction in speed [1 mark] but curve Y shows a large decrease in speed. [1 mark]
   b Dark matter [1 mark]
   c Evidence of the effect of dark matter (due to its mass/gravitational effect) [1 mark]
   d Dark energy [1 mark]